Out of the Box

Out of the Box

Strategies for Achieving
Profits Today and Growth Tomorrow
through Web Services

John Hagel III

HARVARD BUSINESS SCHOOL PRESS
BOSTON, MASSACHUSETTS

Requests for permission to use or reproduce material from this book should be directed to permissions@hbsp.harvard.edu, or mailed to Permissions, Harvard Business School Publishing, 60 Harvard Way, Boston, Massachusetts 02163.

Library of Congress Cataloging-in-Publication Data

Hagel, John.
   Out of the box : strategies for achieving profits today and growth tomorrow through web services / John Hagel III.
      p. cm.
   Includes index.
   ISBN 1-57851-680-3
   1. Electronic commerce. 2. World Wide Web. I. Title.
HF5548.32 .H343 2002
658.8'4—dc21

2002007488

The paper used in this publication meets the requirements of the American National Standard for Permanence of Paper for Publications and Documents in Libraries and Archives Z39.48-1992.

To my mother and father,
Evelyn Hagel and John Hagel Jr.
Their love, support, and encouragement
helped me out of many more boxes
than they will ever know.

Contents

Foreword

OUT OF THE BOX is a deceptive book. It is deceptive because the simplicity and clarity of the writing may mislead the reader. Seduced by the ease of reading, the reader may fail to appreciate the power and insight available throughout the book. In reading this book, I am reminded of Oliver Wendell Holmes's famous observation: "I would not give a fig for the simplicity this side of complexity, but I would give my life for the simplicity on the other side of complexity." John Hagel has fully absorbed the complexity and subtlety of the business and technology issues he addresses, but he communicates it to the reader in a remarkably simple and accessible style.

This book takes a new generation of technology—Web services—and powerfully explores the profound business impact of the technology. Unlike Web sites, which were designed to connect people with resources on the Internet, Web services help to connect business resources (particularly, applications and data) with each other. At one level, this is a very mundane task. It is difficult to write headlines about automated connections. John makes a persuasive case, however, that it is exactly this pragmatism that makes the technology so compelling.

We have just come through a remarkable bubble of information technology (IT) investment. The rate of growth in IT investment in the United States almost doubled in the final half of the 1990s relative to the first half of the 1990s. In some cases, the extravagant promises of new Internet-related technology led otherwise rational managers and investors around the world to pour billions of dollars into business initiatives with no plausible business case. In other cases, large enterprises embarked upon massive enterprise application implementations that consumed substantial resources but more often than not fell far short in terms of delivering anticipated cost savings. This IT investment bubble led to an understandable backlash among business executives, who are now extremely skeptical about any hype surrounding new technologies. The recessionary aftermath of the IT investment bubble has made executives even more suspicious of grand, long-term views of technology potential. If a technology doesn't produce clear near-term cost savings in a relatively short period with a relatively modest investment, executives will quickly lose interest.

This is precisely the economic proposition driving Web services technology into the corporation. While technologists talk eloquently about such grandiose, long-term visions as the dynamic composition of applications from dozens of microservices, something quite different is capturing the attention of business executives. Facing increasing competitive and economic pressures, businesses are desperate to deliver operating cost and asset savings to the bottom line quickly. Web services help businesses to capture these savings by connecting IT resources in a much more pragmatic way than has any previous generation of technology.

Web services begin by honoring the diversity of IT platforms already in place within the enterprise. They recognize that companies have spent a lot of money to accumulate these platforms over time. The last thing executives want to do is rip out any of these platforms and walk away from investments they have already made. They want instead to extract more business value from the platforms already in place. Web services technology can overlay existing platforms, thereby helping to connect, rather than replace, the platforms.

Because the implementation of these overlays is relatively simple, they can be deployed quickly and with modest investment. More conventional integration technologies are much more complex, requiring deeper knowledge of the underlying resources to be connected, and are therefore more expensive and time-consuming to implement. Since these integration technologies are as a rule highly customized to the individual resources being connected, the significant investment required cannot be amortized across a broad range of diverse resources. In contrast, Web services technology overlays can interact with a broad range of other resources, helping to increase the flexibility of the connections and amortize the initial investment as more connections are established. The result is that Web services technology allows a business to economically combine more resources in more ways, thereby generating more value from existing resources.

Web services technology can also be implemented incrementally. Executives can finely target the implementation of the technology to address the high-impact needs of the business. This speeds up implementation and helps to deliver large economic benefits more quickly, building support for future waves of implementation of the technology in other parts of the enterprise. In this way, economic benefits can be more closely tied to the investments required.

It is precisely this pragmatism that makes Web services technology so compelling in this economic environment. No grand visions of the future. No commitment to the revolutionary transformation of business, regardless of the costs. Instead, Web services technology provides simple connections, established in a quick and cost-effective manner, to address significant inefficiencies in business today. Most important, Web services quickly deliver real savings to the bottom line—a breath of fresh air for executives under growing pressure to improve the near-term performance of their companies. Having spent many years as the head of Xerox's Palo Alto Research Center (PARC), I have personally learned the hard way to appreciate the importance of pragmatism in driving technology adoption and what happens when this factor is ignored.

For those concerned about our macroeconomic condition, the pragmatic properties of this new generation of technology may hold the key to our next wave of economic growth. Web services technology produces real business value. It may therefore provide the basis for reviving not only the technology sector, but the rest of the economy as well. The growth of all sectors will be enhanced by the coevolution of the technology and the business practices required to unleash a spiral of increasing economic value.

This pragmatic case for the adoption of Web services technology alone would be enough to make this book required reading for all business executives. But *Out of the Box* does not stop there. It puts this new generation of technology in a broader business context, helping executives to appreciate its real power.

I have written extensively about the dangers of tunnel vision with regard to technology. Too often we find that technology enthusiasts become obsessed with the capabilities of a technology and fail to see or appreciate the broader social context in which technology is used. In the extreme, this tunnel vision can lead to enormous destruction of economic value, as we witnessed in the bursting of the dot-com bubble. Unrealistic expectations created out of context inevitably lead to major reversals as reality eventually delivers its harsh message: Context matters. The risk of tunnel vision applies to Web services technology as well. The only way to reduce this risk is to honor context. This is something that John does throughout the book.

John understands that businesses operate in an environment characterized by increasing complexity, uncertainty, and accelerating change. Web services can provide an important tool for coping with these challenges. They create the foundation for a new type of much more loosely coupled, and therefore flexible, information technology architecture. To provide an enduring foundation, however, providers of these technologies must resist the temptation to build in too many features at the outset. The power of these technologies is precisely their ability to provide simple and flexible ways to connect potentially complex systems. Too many features at the outset will only reduce flexibility. Excess features will also increase barriers to adoption because of the learning curve required to implement the technology. CIOs and CTOs would do well instead to find the simplest way to deliver value at the outset. They could then let the technologies evolve and add features organically and incrementally, with an eye to the diverse experiences within a variety of business contexts.

This evolutionary approach requires a fundamentally different mental model. When confronted with complexity and uncertainty today, most managers fall back on a highly mechanistic mental model. In their minds, the best way to cope with uncertainty is to tighten control over all the elements required for success. Managers seek this tighter control to define in advance and in fine detail all the activities required in challenging environments. Tighter control also enables managers to closely monitor the activities as they are performed and to intervene when deviations from plan occur. At its foundation, this approach to complexity and uncertainty embodies a top-down, mechanistic approach to technology and business. In practice, the approach paradoxically creates brittle systems that often fail when faced with unexpected events.

The loosely coupled architectures enabled by Web services technology start with the assumption that robustness—the ability to perform in highly complex and uncertain environments—requires greater flexibility. Systems must be able to respond to unanticipated events and facilitate real-time changes to continue to perform well. Loosely coupled connections must replace hardwired connections wherever possible. In this way, individual elements within the system can rapidly adapt and exploit opportunities without forcing a redesign of the entire system. Rather than representing a top-down, mechanistic approach, these architectures assume a much more bottom-up, organic approach. This organic approach is much more respectful of context. It does not assume that planners or designers can anticipate the range of needs that will emerge over time. The paradoxical implication is that the best way to cope with uncertainty may be to loosen control rather than tighten control.

As John clearly suggests, loosely coupled architectures enabled by Web services technology will generate minimal economic value if implemented in isolation. To exploit the flexibility created by the new technology architectures, a business needs a very different approach to business process management. Again, such a shift requires a different mental model. John effectively hammers the business process reengineering movement of the 1990s for perpetuating, and even reinforcing, conventional mechanistic mental models. Evolutionary mental models will lead managers to explore the potential of much more loosely coupled approaches to business process management.

John and I both see this as leading to a very different kind of business strategy and corporate landscape. *Out of the Box* discusses some elements of this transformation, especially in terms of the unbundling of the enterprise and the move to more leveraged growth strategies. We are collaborating on further research that will explore these implications in greater detail, and we plan to write a book on our findings.

In brief, our work in this area starts with the assumption that evolutionary mental models require a different approach to design. Design, in a complex and an uncertain world, becomes a shaping philosophy. Rather than accepting a passive posture and simply reacting to changes in the business landscape, shaping strategies seek to understand the underlying forces molding the business landscape. Executives use shaping strategies to craft targeted interventions intended to shift evolutionary trajectories in more favorable directions. Shapers understand that specific outcomes will vary widely but that the probabilities of certain directions can be influenced by actions taken by participants. Of course, not all actions have equivalent influence. The challenge in shaping strategies is to amplify the impact of actions by understanding and targeting key leverage points in the business landscape.

Out of the Box begins to focus on some of these leverage points in its discussion of process networks and the even broader notion of economic webs. Both of these concepts focus on the opportunity to create complex networks of loosely coupled business relationships spanning across a broad range of enterprises. Our research strategy going forward focuses on the trust strategies and incentive mechanisms that will become increasingly critical to the formation and evolution of these relationships. Trust can often take a long time to develop, but the design of incentive mechanisms can significantly expand the scope of trust and accelerate its development. A variety of safety nets and fallback mechanisms can also help facilitate the emergence of trust. Deeper, broader, and faster development of trust can be a powerful way to mobilize a vast array of resources to support specific business strategies.

The creative use of trust strategies and incentive mechanisms will set the stage for a fundamental reshaping of the business landscape. A key element of this reshaping will be the emergence of a much higher degree of specialization and focus in enterprises than we have ever seen. Adam Smith's *Wealth of Nations* welcomed the virtues of the division of labor, but more than two hundred years later, our enterprises still span a broad range of business activities. The emergence of process networks and economic webs will accelerate and reinforce a trend toward increasing specialization at the enterprise level. Some prognosticators anticipate that every individual will become a "free agent" liberated from the shackles of the enterprise. We adopt a more nuanced view, recognizing that enterprises and other organizational forms continue to have value in integrating communities of practice and developing the skills of an organization's employees.

Specialization at the enterprise level will give rise to a much richer and more diverse ecology of businesses. This specialization will help to accelerate performance improvement as enterprises are freed to focus on the areas where they truly have the potential for world-class performance. Performance will be further enhanced by the emergence and evolution of *learning ecologies*—networks of businesses coming together expressly for the purpose of strengthening the flow of knowledge. The cross-pollination of knowledge will require the development of new learning mechanisms, supported and reinforced by appropriate incentive mechanisms—creating both the will and the capability to rapidly improve performance. This link between accelerated learning and incentives created by "win-win" economic games will provide the foundation of value creation in the future.

Out of the Box, true to its title, helps us break out of the mental models and other barriers holding us back. It does this by taking complex topics and reducing them to simple principles, providing an enduring foundation for the journey ahead. It points us in the right direction and provides valuable advice on how to proceed, particularly in the early stages of our journey. By following its counsel, executives will be able to generate significant value. The challenge for all of us over time will be to develop a deeper understanding of the practices required to create and capture even more economic value. These practices will be deeply embedded in our daily work and the fabric of our organizations. We are only now beginning to appreciate how profoundly these practices will need to change to capture the full range of opportunities that reside well out of the box. Before we can embark on these more fundamental changes, we will first need to master the insight and thinking captured so eloquently in this book.

John Seely Brown

Acknowledgments

OUT OF THE BOX represents the latest stop on a long journey. More than twenty years ago, I became fascinated with the complex interplay between information technology and business performance. Over the years, many people influenced my thinking and shaped my experiences, often in ways that neither they nor I understood at the time. I could not hope to acknowledge all their contributions over these past decades.

Let me be content with trying to acknowledge at least some of the people who were most helpful in shaping the development of this book. One individual stands out above all the rest. I have known John Seely Brown for many years and deeply admired and respected his insight in an extraordinary array of disciplines and interests. It is only in the past two years that I have had the privilege of working closely with him on a professional level. In those two years, I have benefited enormously from our collaboration. Much of the thinking in the pages ahead has been profoundly shaped by our discussions and joint research and writing initiatives. We both share a deep conviction that we are only at the earliest stages of understanding the widespread changes brought about by the coevolution of technology innovation and business strategy. I look forward to many more years of collaboration with John in exploring these changes.

More broadly, I have benefited from the deep insight into Web services technology that I gained by working with 12 Entrepreneuring, Inc. In particular, Halsey Minor drove home to me the importance of starting simple and moving in rapid increments. The individuals behind Grand Central, including Craig Donato, Ken Norton, Jason Douglas, Ron Palmeri, and Adam Gross, provided me with an increased appreciation of the importance of a service grid in Web services architectures. Mahmoud Falaki, Martin Milani, and Vivek Shivpuri patiently tutored me in the subtleties of technology architectures. Sam Parker kept trying to tie everything back to implications for entrepreneurial ventures. My fellow McKinsey & Company alumni, Scott Durchslag and Dennis Layton-Rodin, provided valuable sounding boards and research support. Kevin Scher and Sunwoo Hwang contributed both research support and repeated challenges, forcing me to sharpen my own thinking. David Beirne underscored in more ways than one that the success of business ultimately depends far more on the people than on the business concept.

Some of my early thinking on the themes in *Out of the Box* began when I was still at McKinsey & Company. In that context, I have a broad range of indebtedness to many people, including, but certainly not limited to, Jonathan Auerbach, Byron Auguste, Carter Bales, Eric Beinhocker, Jed Dempsey, Dick Foster, Ted Hall, Detlev Hoch, Rod Laird, Will Lansing, James Manyika, Bill Matassoni, Lenny Mendonca, Mike Nevens, Ken Ohmae, Marc Singer, Somu Subramaniam, and Tom Woodard. These people helped shape my "personal McKinsey" and kept me honest while at the same time challenging me to push the envelope of my own thinking. Lang Davison not only kept me honest and challenged my thinking—he taught me how to write more clearly and compellingly.

Even more broadly, I continue to be strongly influenced by the work on complex adaptive systems at the Santa Fe Institute. In particular, Brian Arthur, John Holland, Stuart Kauffman, and John Padgett have each shaped my thinking in important ways. The business world has just begun to understand the application of complex adaptive systems insights to business.

Many early adopters of Web services technology and related innovative business practices helped me to see both the opportunities and the challenges ahead. Mark Hogan, president of eGM; Eric Michlowitz, Dell's director of supply-chain e-business solutions; John McKinley, CTO of Merrill Lynch; and Sue Bostrom, senior vice president of Internet Business Solutions at Cisco, in particular provided me with invaluable access to real-world experience in extracting business value from new technology. Victor Fung, chairman of Li & Fung, provided compelling personal evidence that companies can be leading-edge innovators of business practices without necessarily being at the leading edge of information technology adoption.

Nick Carr at *Harvard Business Review* was one of the first to see the business importance of Web services technology. He helped John Seely Brown and me to produce one of the first business perspectives on the adoption of Web services technology. Kirsten Sandberg at Harvard Business School Press has now been involved with the editing of three of my books—they are far better than they ever would have been without her thoughtful comments and deep insight into the material. Most important, Kirsten's great enthusiasm and confidence in me sustained me during a period when endless distractions and extraordinary stress seemed certain to sabotage the writing of this book.

Carrie Howell, my assistant and "command center," has also been with me through the writing of three of my books. She has followed me from the safety of McKinsey & Company, through the turmoil that marked our sojourn at 12 Entrepreneuring, and now into the glorious freedom of a career as an independent consultant and author. Throughout it all, Carrie has provided invaluable support. I would be truly lost without her.

Most important of all, there is my wife, Jane, and our two children, Rachel and Rebecca. They have provided me with the safe harbor and the encouragement to pursue my passions. Their love makes everything seem possible and makes our home an incredibly energizing place.

Of course, the plight of the author is that ultimately all responsibility for the perspectives advanced on the pages ahead rests with me. I continue to prefer the perils of speculation to the safety of the present. I accept all the risks that a speculative path encounters. The rewards more than make up for these risks.

Out of the Box

PART I

Finding Flexibility

1

Responding to Unmet Needs

CORPORATE MANAGERS around the world know stress. They know, understand, live with, and somehow cope with growing stress in all aspects of their work. Never before has the Red Queen's observation from Lewis Carroll's *Through the Looking-Glass* seemed so relevant: You need to run faster and faster, just to stay in the same place.

Much of the stress can be attributed to intensifying competition. Technology innovation and market liberalization in the 1980s and 1990s have combined to make the management task more challenging than ever before. Uncertainty prevails, margins are relentlessly squeezed as customers gain more power, and growth becomes a necessity rather than a luxury.

One result is that even large companies find it harder to sustain position. The average time a company spends on the Standard & Poor's 500 has steadily declined since the 1940s. This decline is only exceeded by the shortening of the average tenure of a corporate manager. Advancing in the corporate hierarchy offers no greater security. Quite the contrary. Senior executives are even more exposed. Turnover among CEOs is at an all-time high.

This corporate instability can be stressful enough, but there is a second kind of stress that compounds the first. It is the stress of seeing a storm approach, of knowing that its impact will be brutal and yet that one has limited ability to respond. We are all familiar with the nightmare of a rapidly approaching predator. In the dream, we try to run as hard as possible, only to find that we move in slow motion while the predator gains on us. That nightmare has become a daily reality for many of us. It is the paradox of the Red Queen— we exert increasing energy trying to move faster, but the reality is that we are barely changing position.

We have the claustrophobic feeling of being trapped in a box— and it's not just one box, but boxes within boxes (figure 1-1). Mounting financial performance pressures define the broadest kind of box. Caught between eroding margins and slowing growth, we desperately try to fix one or the other. We all have been taught that scaling back on growth plans and focusing on streamlining current operations is the best way to address the pressures of achieving near-term profitability. More recently, we became seduced by the prospect that we could ignore near-term profitability issues as long as we could deliver high rates of growth. Focus on growth, and somehow profitability would take care of itself. Financial markets deliver a different message: Managers must deliver both profits and growth.

Operational and organizational infrastructures within the enterprise represent a second kind of box. We simply can't move as flexibly as we would like. We run in slow motion as the predators approach because we are trapped by inflexible infrastructures. Information technology (IT) systems today represent a significant source of inflexibility. These systems seriously restrict the freedom of movement needed to respond to unanticipated events in the environment. They also represent a significant drag on both cost reduction and growth. A business can achieve large, one-time reductions in operating cost and asset investment through painful and expensive changes to its core IT platforms. The problem is that today's intensifying competition demands more than large, one-time improvements in efficiency. Corporations must be able to continuously improve their efficiency in substantial increments just to stay in the game. Inflexible IT systems can significantly slow down these efforts.

The business process reengineering movement that gripped the imagination of business executives around the world in the early 1990s promised radical improvements in performance, but all it really did was reengineer the same box. In part, this was not the fault of the methodology; it reflected the limitations of the existing IT systems. Yes, you could reengineer major business processes to

FIGURE 1 - 1

Four Management Boxes

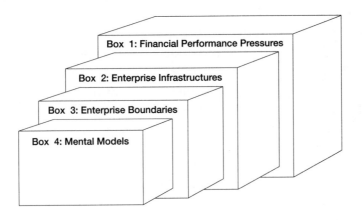

make them more efficient, but you would need massive investments to implement the IT systems required. What you got at the end of the effort was typically another rigid set of platforms that were difficult to improve further. Given the effort required and the results achieved, this reengineering was not something executives (much less the rest of the company) wanted to undertake very often.

Growth can be just as challenging within the confines of this second box. Organic growth usually comes through introducing new products, adding of new sales channels, or targeting new customer segments. Any of these initiatives typically require significant modifications to supporting IT systems. The inflexibility of these systems at best imposes significant lead times in the implementation of these growth initiatives. More than one large telecommunications company has had to forgo the introduction of innovative services because it could not make cost-effective changes to its billing system for these new services. If a company seeks to grow through mergers and acquisitions, then postmerger integration of IT systems can often become a major obstacle to achieving anticipated operating efficiencies. IT systems that were supposed to liberate business and expand options have instead become another box, tightly constraining the freedom of movement within the enterprise.

The boundaries of our enterprises represent a third kind of box. We all know the rhetoric of collaboration. To enhance performance, we need to work more closely with a broader range of business partners. Working with these partners, we can increase efficiency in business processes that span multiple enterprises. These business partners can also help us accelerate growth by providing access to a broader array of resources than what exists within any individual enterprise. These are fine concepts until some business manager, carried away by the rhetoric, actually tries to make these concepts operational. Countless obstacles stand in the way.

Again, business process reengineering, while presenting itself as a revolutionary approach to delivering higher performance, has really operated much too comfortably within the box. Proponents of business process reengineering would often talk about the importance of taking an end-to-end view of business processes. When they discussed examples, though, it became abundantly clear that their end-to-end view usually stopped at the edge of the enterprise. More enlightened proponents would occasionally include direct business partners of the enterprise. None expanded the notion of end-to-end to include the entire value chain, extending from raw materials to the finished products and services used by consumers. The boundaries of the enterprise were simply too formidable for even the so-called revolutionaries to breach.

IT systems again play a key role in defining this box. Not only are IT systems remarkably inflexible within the enterprise, but they are also very difficult and expensive to connect across enterprises. In the absence of IT connections, the edges of our enterprises have become gathering points for significant operating inefficiency and accumulations of excess working capital. So-called swivel-chair integration, whereby a person manually outputs data from one company's application and then manually reenters it into another company's application, becomes the weak link of collaboration. Where IT connections are established across enterprises, they become just as difficult to modify as a company's internal IT systems. We are all familiar with the notion of functional silos fragmenting the enterprise, with barriers to coordination across functions like marketing and sales created by incompatible IT systems or organizational structures. Many companies have spent significant money to break down functional silos within the enterprise only to find that the enterprise silo represents the next big barrier to performance improvement.

Finally, there is the most insidious box of all. This is the box that we all create in terms of the mind-sets we bring to our businesses. Even if we were able to be much more flexible and collaborative in our business operations, we would have a hard time exploiting that capability. We all have built up a large set of assumptions about what is possible and what is required for success. We take many of these assumptions for granted and even have a hard time articulating them if asked. Yet these assumptions play a significant role in constraining our options, especially if they are broadly shared among the management team. It just doesn't occur to us that there might be another way to approach an opportunity or challenge. In fact, we may not even see the opportunity or challenge to begin with, since these assumptions also shape the lens we apply in seeing and interpreting our surroundings. Broadly speaking, managers tend to be most comfortable with mechanistic mental models: Develop detailed blueprints, and then micromanage activities.

The advocates of business process reengineering challenged conventional business practices, but at the end of the day, they remained firmly within a mechanistic mental model. Even the language they used shaped, and revealed, their outlook. *Reengineering*—could one possibly choose a more mechanistic, top-down, deterministic view of business activities? It is not surprising that this movement remained tightly focused on the enterprise. Such a model operates best when there is, at least theoretically, a single decision maker at the top who can impose designs and micromanage activities. How could one possibly reengineer a business process that extends across multiple levels of activity and may involve hundreds, if not thousands, of independent enterprises? A completely different mental model, not to mention different tools and methodologies, would be required. The view of orchestration and process networks developed in the final part of this book begins to offer an alternative way of thinking about business processes— much more flexible and far-reaching than the end-to-end processes residing within a single enterprise. In this view, even the notion of end-to-end becomes much too confining. It suggests a linear view of business processes that misses the richness of increasingly diverse, highly specialized enterprises coming together in tailored configurations to deliver optimal value to individual customers.

To exploit the opportunities emerging on the horizon, managers will need to shift to very different mental models of evolutionary change: Start quickly and simply, and then flexibly adjust actions based on new information and knowledge. Thinking out of the box may be the first necessary step to extricating ourselves from the other boxes.

The Red Queen rules within these boxes. The treadmill moves ever faster, and we move ever slower. The challenge—and opportunity—will be to move outside the boxes. As suggested by the cover illustration of this book, the movement outside the boxes will be far more steady and deliberate. Managers will be able to mobilize their assets, rather than remain trapped by them. What is most important, the economic rewards will be substantial.

A Catalyst for Breaking Out of the Box

This book cannot eliminate the stress caused by competition that continues to intensify—*that* stress is here to stay. Readers of this book, however, can significantly reduce the second form of stress—the feeling of being trapped in a box. By providing managers with more degrees of freedom, this book can help managers break out of the boxes that limit options. In doing so, managers can relieve, but certainly not eliminate, the inevitable stress that competitive markets create.

The bottom line is that managers need to develop more flexibility and collaboration capability to deliver continuing rounds of operating cost and asset savings as well as accelerating growth. They need to escape from the high cost and inflexible infrastructures that make both cost reduction and growth such daunting challenges.

This book discusses how a new generation of IT and related architectures—known generally as Web services technology and distributed service architectures—will provide a significant catalyst in helping management break out of the boxes that confine it today. Web services are often confused with Web sites or with a type of business known as application service providers (ASPs). The first generation of the World Wide Web was about connecting people to Web sites. Web services technology inaugurates the second generation by focusing on automating connections across applications and data without human intervention. As discussed in chapter 3, ASPs emerged in the late 1990s and largely represented an effort to make traditional application software available to a broader range of customers by adopting a "rental" pricing model and a shared-services delivery model. Since Web services are also made available to users as shared services, people often equate ASPs with Web services. ASPs, however, generally relied on very traditional software technologies to deliver their services and encountered significant difficulties as a result. Web services technology addresses many of the challenges encountered by ASPs.

Web services technology offers a very different approach to generating business value from IT. It does not require the removal of the extensive IT infrastructures that have accumulated within companies over decades. Instead, it provides an overlay that can help to more effectively connect IT platforms to provide more value for the business. These connections can be established more quickly, more flexibly, and in a more cost-effective way than could previous generations of technology. Of course, a connecting overlay like this can substantially reduce IT development and operating costs. But that is a small part of the business value. The real value is the increased capability of business managers for flexibility and collaboration—capabilities that can in turn produce significant operating savings and growth options across the entire business. In particular, enterprises can achieve significant economic value by finding new ways for companies to work together—both to eliminate the substantial inefficiency that currently plagues connections across companies and to mobilize a broader range of resources to deliver more value to customers.

Not to worry—this is not a technology book. If we have learned one thing since the 1980s, it is that information technology is at best a catalyst and an enabler. It is never an answer in itself. For too long, we have bought each new generation of technology, eager to reap significant economic rewards, only to find that the rewards often fall short of expectations. In far too many cases, we even find that all we have done is to add more operating cost and capital expense to our business, without any corresponding performance improvement or return on investment.

In fact, many executives use information technology as an excuse for inaction. As already indicated, technology can be a barrier to more rapid movement, but substantial progress can often be made without the help of new information technology. Later parts of this book will discuss examples of companies that have launched major restructuring programs and adopted innovative approaches to business process management without requiring significant infusions of new technology. Information technology can augment or amplify such business initiatives, but it rarely blocks all movement. Executives who are creative in reshaping their business and organization more broadly will be most able to exploit the potential of new information technology as it becomes available.

The next chapter will provide enough of a foundation in the new technology to help managers understand why it is so distinctive and powerful. The real focus of the book, though, is on the business impact of the technology. A key theme is that the introduction of the technology into the business will enhance the ability to systematically overhaul the management approach to the business. Managers will need to aggressively rethink and redesign their business to harness the real economic potential of this technology. Those who understand this and who avoid the temptation to inject the technology into the business without changing the business will reap the real economic rewards.

What are the real economic rewards? In the near term, the adoption of Web services technology will be driven by the quest for savings in operating costs and assets. The value proposition will be powerful and hard to resist: Relatively modest investments in new Web services overlays can deliver tangible operating savings with very short lead times. As economic pressures mount, this pragmatic proposition will contribute to a rapid adoption of this new generation of technology.

But these early economic rewards can be deceptive. They can lead managers to view the technology as simply one more tool to do things faster and cheaper, but not materially change the nature or direction of the business. Such a view is dangerous since it can blind managers to the real economic value of the technology. In delivering near-term operating savings, Web services technology creates the potential for much greater flexibility and collaboration in business operations. Managers who understand this and move aggressively to exploit this capability will find that they can substantially accelerate business growth. Even better, they will be able to grow rapidly by mobilizing assets owned by other enterprises, delivering more value to their customers with modest asset commitments of their own. This leveraged growth opportunity is the real economic prize offered by this next generation of technology.

Realizing this economic prize will require fundamental changes to business process management and organizations, building on the unique capabilities of the new technology. At the end of the day, it will even call into play the most basic questions of all: What business are we really in? What is the nature of the enterprise?

Before the jaded reader develops an allergic reaction to the change-the-world tone, let's quickly flag another key theme running throughout the book. The theme is not about massive, overnight change. The pragmatism of this new generation of technology stems from its ability to leverage existing assets and surgically slice through the enterprise. This is not a call for creating new businesses on a greenfield basis. Instead, the idea is to take existing businesses and reshape them a step at a time to unleash more value from the assets already in place. Managers can target very narrow parts of the business for early deployments of the technology and proceed incrementally through the rest of the enterprise.

We have all grown tired of the change-the-world promises of new technology. There is one key difference this time. In the past, managers were presented compelling visions of the new world that awaited, but there was a price to be paid—massive investment over extended periods of time. For those patient enough and wealthy enough to stay the course, the new world would be wonderful.

Now, the proposition is far more pragmatic: Invest modest sums, and focus on near-term economic returns. In fact, insist upon near-term results. Don't move forward unless these returns materialize. When these returns do begin to appear, recognize that the intensifying competition will force you to keep moving and to expand the implementation of this technology while at the same time you rethink the business to generate even more near-term economic returns. Over time, the cumulative impact will be profound, but don't adopt the technology for that reason. Adopt it because it will help you to achieve near-term business objectives.

By adhering to these guidelines—use technology as a catalyst to overhaul management approaches, target near-term profits and long-term growth, and proceed pragmatically in rapid increments—managers can escape the boxes that have held them captive. Managers can harness the enhanced flexibility and collaboration capability intrinsic to this new technology by making the corresponding changes in their management approaches. This flexibility and collaboration capability can then be deployed to deliver both near-term profitability and longer-term growth opportunities.

Existing management mind-sets represent the one remaining box that can still prevent all this from occurring. This book represents one small step in a much broader effort necessary to shift management mind-sets. By helping managers to think out of the box, this book seeks to help them escape from the boxes that make life not only challenging, but also frustrating. Managers must first see the potential of the new generation of technology. They must then be prepared to act, often in very new and unfamiliar ways, to realize that potential.

The incremental adoption of the technology represents good news and bad news. The good news is that it provides managers with some reasonable runway to evolve their mind-sets. Existing mind-sets can migrate over time, much as the technology will migrate, progressively realizing the broader potential offered by the technology. The bad news is that the early stages of deployment of the technology can look deceptively simple and mundane—tackling operating savings in modest increments. These modest beginnings can lull management into a sense of complacency. Managers can miss the magnitude of the opportunity and lose valuable time in building the capability to exploit the opportunity. Management mind-sets in the end will determine who creates value with Web services technology and who destroys value by failing to exploit this technology aggressively enough.

The Migration Path

Early efforts to deploy Web services technology have been highly opportunistic. Line managers confront a pressing business problem and are frustrated that existing technology cannot resolve the problem. Somehow, they hear about this intriguing new generation of technology called Web services and find some people who can help them implement the technology. As we will see in later chapters, the business results from these early initiatives are quite impressive.

But, there's a problem. These early initiatives are completely ad hoc. They depend on a chance connection between someone with a problem and people who have enough familiarity with a very new technology to address the problem. There is no assurance that these early initiatives are targeting the most pressing opportunities for the application of this new technology. There is also the risk that these ad hoc initiatives will rapidly multiply within the enterprise as word spreads, without anyone making the effort to build upon the learning already achieved or to focus resources on the highest-impact areas.

In parallel, many IT groups are beginning to examine Web services technology and explore its long-term potential for redefining the technology architectures of the enterprise. These top-down efforts rarely focus on tangible, near-term business initiatives. To the extent that a migration path has been defined, it is usually driven by ease of implementation rather than size of business impact.

Managers need a broad view of how Web services technology might be deployed. This view must be shaped by both a high-level view of the long-term opportunities and a much more textured view of the specific near-term opportunities that can drive real economic impact. The view needs to be firmly grounded in an understanding of both the capabilities and limitations of the technology. It must also understand the capabilities and limitations of the business. Even more than they need a migration path for the technology, managers need a migration path for the business.

Part 1 of this book, consisting of this chapter and the next, provides a brief overview of the opportunity and a foundation in the technology that will serve as a catalyst for exploiting the opportunity. As chapter 2 makes clear, Web services technology is still at an early stage of development. A number of major obstacles stand in the path of development and could ultimately undermine the potential opportunity. Managers need to understand these obstacles and monitor efforts to overcome them. Parts 2 through 4 map out a high-level management view of a migration path that

FIGURE 1 - 2

The Web Services Migration Path

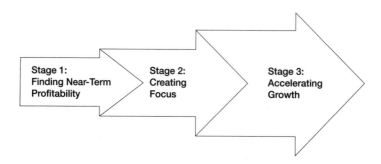

captures the economic value available from this new technology. These three parts map to the three broad stages of value creation and capture—finding near-term profitability, creating focus, and accelerating growth (figure 1-2).

Finding Near-Term Profitability

Part 2, Finding Near-Term Profitability, summarizes the early experience with the adoption of Web services. It identifies a pragmatic adoption path based on the patterns emerging from these early experiences. Early adopters have leveraged existing technology investments and moved incrementally. By structuring their initiatives around tangible early wins, they have delivered quantifiable operating savings. They also are realistic about the current capabilities of the technology. They understand its limitations today and work around these limitations by combining other technologies where appropriate in their initiatives to supplement the functionality of Web services technology.

The pace of adoption of Web services will be determined by how quickly these limitations in functionality are overcome. Because technology companies are investing billions of dollars in the development of Web services technology, we have reason to be optimistic that these limitations will be rapidly addressed. Part 2 identifies and explores some of the key factors determining the pace of adoption, providing managers with some context to evaluate the progression of the technology.

Given the capabilities and economics of Web services technology, early adoption tends to concentrate at the edge of the enterprise, where business processes need to interact with many other enterprises. It is exactly here, in functions like sales and procurement, that the limitations of existing technologies are most evident. It is also here that businesses can achieve significant near-term operating savings by tackling the inefficiencies in business processes spanning multiple enterprises.

Although adoption will begin at the edge of the enterprise, it will spread inexorably into the core of the enterprise. A variety of paths will draw Web services into the core. In some cases, Web services will follow business processes from the edge back into the enterprise. In other cases, Web services will spread through administrative processes like human resource management or financial management. One of the most interesting potential applications for Web services will be to accelerate the delivery of near-term operating savings from postmerger integration. Independent software vendors will also begin to play a role as they start using Web services technology to create more flexibility for themselves and for their customers. Over time, distributed service architectures enabled by Web services technology have the potential to become the dominant technology architecture for all business activities.

Creating Focus

As Web services technology spreads throughout the enterprise, business managers will at least have the potential for much greater flexibility. But technology is not the only barrier to flexibility. Over the years, the business world has built up massive organizational infrastructures and management practices based on the assumption that businesses do not have a lot of flexibility. These infrastructures and practices will need to be systematically broken apart and rebuilt if Web services technology is to deliver more value. Part 3 of this book, Creating Focus, examines how this might be done and what might emerge in terms of new infrastructures and practices.

Again, the primary driver of this reconfiguration, at least at the outset, is likely to be the pressure for even greater operating efficiency. Managers have an opportunity to apply a very different approach to the management of business processes, especially as these processes span multiple enterprises. The orchestration of process networks offers a much more flexible way of managing business processes than does the traditional approach. It makes it easier to tailor a business process to the needs of specific products, customers, or transactions. But that is only the beginning. The real power of this orchestration approach will be to foster opportunities for specialization and rapid performance improvement among the participants. To exploit this potential, managers will need to develop a different focus on business processes, understanding that the processes do not begin and end at the boundaries of the enterprise, but instead reach out to encompass and mobilize a very diverse set of enterprises.

The increasing importance of process networks will be accompanied by another broad trend that will significantly restructure the enterprise itself. Enterprises today represent a tightly integrated bundle of three very different kinds of businesses as described in chapter 7. These three business types have been bundled together in large part because of the difficulties in establishing flexible connections across enterprises. We have already begun to see some unbundling, but this new generation of technology will significantly accelerate this trend. Web services technology will give managers much greater ability to focus on one of these three businesses while increasingly relying on other enterprises that focus on the other two types of businesses. Not only will they be able to focus tightly, but as competitive pressures intensify, they will *have* to do so to deliver world-class performance to their customers. Although this might appear to be a case for shrinking the enterprise, the opposite is the case. It creates a new, more focused platform for significant growth.

Focus will be essential to deal with the very real stress managers feel as they try to cope with increased information and an expanding array of business options. With so much noise and so few reliable filters, some managers simply cannot tolerate the complexity. In this respect, the boxes outlined previously begin to have a seductive appeal, offering the illusion of a safety zone where difficult choices need not be confronted. To help managers operate successfully out of the box, businesses will need to become increasingly clear about their tighter focus on areas in which they can be truly world-class.

Committing to a tighter focus will require managers to rethink notions of business risk. Just as we came to realize that diversified conglomerates tend to create more business risk by spreading management attention too thinly across very different businesses, we need to realize that this applies to most of our tightly bundled enterprises today. The biggest risk that managers face today is competition from more focused and more nimble competitors. By unbundling even further into more focused types of business, managers enhance their ability to cope with business risk.

Accelerating Growth

Part 4 makes the case that the real economic value of Web services technology will be realized in the form of innovative growth strategies. In particular, this technology makes it easier for an enterprise to deploy leveraged growth strategies. In the wake of Enron, we are all too familiar with financial leverage strategies that can create significant business risk. Leveraged growth strategies are different—they involve the use of economic incentives to access and mobilize assets owned by other corporations. As a result, enterprises can quickly generate significant additional value for their customers without a corresponding increase in asset investments. These leveraged growth strategies can be built on process networks, but they can also focus on other forms of resource aggregation. Of course, they can also be combined with more traditional forms of growth—organic growth and mergers and acquisitions.

Business growth is the ultimate value creation opportunity offered by Web services technology. But realizing this opportunity will be far from easy. Management will need to develop a very different, and more layered, approach to business strategy, rapidly iterating between longer-term opportunity definition and aggressive, near-term operational initiatives.

Management must also embark on an extended process of layered organizational change. As with the implementation of Web services technology itself, this organizational change should be sequenced and tied to specific near-term operating benchmarks. The early stages of organizational change will focus on building new skills and developing new roles, such as process orchestrators and Web services architects. As the enterprise starts to sharpen its focus, organizational change will concentrate on evolving new organizational structures. Enterprises will create a new, pivotal role—business-type managers—and new structures will be required to support these managers. To exploit the growth opportunities, managers will again need to shift the focus of organizational change to the deployment of new systems: performance measurement, reward, knowledge development, and information systems. Long-term organizational forms are still difficult to predict, but the early needs loom clearly. Managers must address these early needs in order to accelerate movement toward the economic opportunities catalyzed by the technology.

This is the bottom line. We confront a technology that can become a significant catalyst to define and deliver substantial economic opportunities. But it is only a catalyst. The choices we make as managers will determine the scope and nature of the opportunity for our companies. If we make the right choices, we will have a chance to escape from the boxes that frustrate us today. The escape will not be easy—we will be constantly challenged to question conventional assumptions and comfortable practices. Many will not even see the opportunity. They will continue to remain closed in the boxes that make every day more frustrating. Some will see the opportunity but will either try to move too quickly or fail to stay the course. They will blame the technology for its failure to produce results. For those few who succeed, the rewards will make the journey well worth the effort. If we have learned one thing from previous generations of technology, it is that each generation creates a new set of winners in terms of value creation and a new set of losers in terms of destroying economic value. Where we end up will be up to us.

2

Web Services Create
New Options

A WORD OF WARNING. For those readers without technology backgrounds, this chapter may prove challenging. Every effort has been made to reduce the technical jargon, but inevitably a person must master some terminology to communicate with technologists and to understand how a new technology can distinctively solve real business needs. The chapter will, at each step along the way, explicitly seek to tie the technology back to the business context. As we will see, what makes Web services technology so powerful is its distinctive ability to help managers operate more flexibly and collaborate more successfully with business partners.

While large enterprises were rushing to implement massive enterprise resource planning (ERP) applications in the 1990s, a new technology began to emerge outside these large enterprises. Spawned by the Internet, this technology offered a new way to establish much more flexible and low-cost connections across applications. Known as Web services, this new technology is still evolving, but it is already clear that it will play a major role in delivering tangible business value quickly to enterprises of all sizes. For those who have invested heavily in ERP applications, the good news is that a business can use Web services to leverage its earlier investment and create much more flexibility. For those who have not yet implemented ERP applications, there is even better news: There may now be much more focused and accelerated ways to achieve business objectives.

19

Genesis of the Technology

We have heard so much about the Internet in recent years that we often forget that this flexible and rapidly evolving network has only been around since the late 1960s. It is equally remarkable that, in this short life span, the Internet has gone through three major eras and is on the cusp of yet a fourth.

As with many technologies, it can be hard to pinpoint the birth of the Internet. If one takes a fairly broad view of the Internet, 1969 becomes a likely candidate for the birth of this remarkable electronic network. That was the year that Bolt Beranek and Newman (BBN), a computer-engineering firm under contract with the Advanced Research Projects Agency (ARPA) in the Defense Department, connected four universities with an innovative network that went by the name of ARPANET. In this first era of the Internet, the focus was on connecting ARPA-funded computing resources at various research centers in an effort to maximize usage of expensive and highly specialized facilities. In other words, this first era provided more effective connections across geographically dispersed computers.

A second era quickly followed. Three years after ARPANET began operation, BBN developed an electronic mail software program in 1972. Until then, electronic mail had only been available in rudimentary form by people sharing the same computer. Now, people could communicate electronically even though they were using different computers. This application, completely unanticipated at the time of the original development of ARPANET, spread rapidly throughout the network. A network originally conceived to connect machines was now being used increasingly to connect people.

The third era took a bit longer to arrive. In 1991, CERN (Conseil Européen pour la Recherche Nucléaire), a European research laboratory, released the software code required to build World Wide Web servers and browsers. A physicist at CERN had originally developed this software to help researchers share and exchange knowledge across incompatible information technologies. This development launched a decade of massive technology investment, all focused on connecting people through browsers to information and other resources available on Web sites.

The fourth era began in 1997 with the adoption by the World Wide Web Consortium (W3C) of a new standard for defining and naming data. The standard, officially named the eXtensible Markup Language, rapidly became better known by its somewhat eccentric acronym—XML. As a later section of this chapter develops in more detail, XML in many respects returns to the roots of the Internet by focusing on the challenge of helping applications communicate directly with each other. In other words, XML seeks to automate connections across applications. This standard emerged in response to growing technical challenges on the World Wide Web, but its value extends far beyond conventional Web sites. In its broadest application, XML helps connect diverse applications and data of all kinds, targeting the technology foundations of all businesses.

The Problem in Connecting with Others

What was the problem that XML originally sought to address? It had many dimensions, but at its foundation, the problem was how to more efficiently and flexibly connect a growing array of technology resources required to support commercial activity on the Internet. In the process of connecting people to Web sites that would be increasingly helpful, businesses found that more and more applications and data needed to be connected behind the scenes.

Take the example of traditional companies establishing Web sites. Web sites could operate as stand-alone platforms as long as they offered limited information, but they quickly ran into problems when they tried to bring together a broader range of information from different sources or—perish the thought—actually enable users to buy products.

Many of the product distributors setting up Web sites received information on product specs and pricing from hundreds, if not thousands, of product vendors. Organizing this information so that it could be easily searched and compared by customers represented a serious technical challenge. Product vendors supplied the information in their own unique formats. Somehow, these diverse formats had to be converted or translated into a single, uniform format.

Translating diversely formatted information was only the beginning of the challenge. Assume now that the product distributor wanted to sell products to customers online. Customers would want to check a product's availability before placing an order. This requires connecting to an inventory application to confirm availability. The distributor would want to check the credit records of new customers and the authorization levels of existing customers. Such checks require a connection to finance applications and customer records. To place an order, the customer would need to connect into an order-entry system. More and more applications in the enterprise had to be connected to the Web site's electronic commerce application to create a seamless interface for the customer.

In many respects, these challenges were becoming a major roadblock to realizing the original promise of the World Wide Web: to help make products, and information about products, more accessible. Although some companies succeeded in creating the appearance of integration, they did so at enormous cost. For the Internet to achieve its true business potential, additional technology innovation would be required.

What were the technical challenges that had to be addressed? Two big ones stood out. First, there was the so-called n-squared problem, a fancy way to describe the growing costs of complexity in technology integration. If you need to connect two applications, a custom connection can be designed reflecting the specific functionality of each application. Technologists describe this as a point-to-point solution. Now, assume that six applications need to be connected with each other. The expense and effort required to establish connections across these resources doesn't increase linearly with the number of resources. Instead, it increases exponentially—hence, n squared. Technology managers soon found themselves drowning in the escalating costs of complexity.

The high cost of complexity was the dark side of the much-touted network-effect business models on the Internet. Network-effect business models assumed that the value to participants would increase exponentially as more participants joined. These business models had many challenges. One that caught managers by surprise was that due to the n-squared problem operating costs were also rising exponentially as more participants joined. Since many of these business models required a critical mass of participants before distinctive value could be delivered, managers found that the rapidly escalating costs significantly increased the investment required to reach critical mass.

The *n*-squared problem was challenging enough. But that wasn't all. Complicating life even further was the second problem: Web sites were rapidly evolving, adding unforeseen partners and losing others. Managers had very little foresight into the long-term network of relationships required to support the business. The escalating costs of complexity are burdensome if the connections are likely to endure for some time. They become unbearable if the nature and number of the connections are being continually redefined. In environments of rapid change and uncertainty about outcomes, managers have little hope of recouping the substantial investments required to establish connections in the first place.

Existing technology simply wasn't up to the challenges confronted by businesses establishing Web sites with increasing functionality. Conventional technology solutions like electronic data interchange (EDI) networks or early generations of enterprise application integration (EAI) technology focused on establishing point-to-point connections. These technologies were poorly suited to the complex and shifting web of relationships emerging around Internet Web sites. They also assumed that one decision maker had sufficient power to ensure that all participants adopted a common technology infrastructure. As a result, where even feasible, the technologies were very costly to implement, required long lead times to deliver, and were very difficult to modify once established.

In practice, many managers responsible for Internet Web sites opted for a "no tech" solution—often described as swivel-chair integration. Behind the scenes, a growing army of people was manually generating information out of one set of applications or databases, manually converting it into another format, and then inputting the reformatted information into other applications or databases. Not only was this labor-intensive process very expensive, it also was time-consuming and prone to errors. It had the virtue of communicating the illusion of integration to users of the Web site, but it was not sustainable.

Technology at the time simply could not deal adequately with these two problems encountered by companies operating Internet Web sites. In truth, though, the problems faced by these companies were only earlier and perhaps more extreme versions of the problems confronted by all companies as they wrestled with the consequences of intensifying competition. All companies were learning that they needed to find lower-cost and more-flexible ways to connect with a growing array of other companies in order to deliver more value at lower cost to their customers. As a result, the technology that emerged to address the problems arising on the Internet had a much broader range of application. All companies over time would find value in solving the n-squared problem and the problem of the increasing change and uncertainty in connections across applications and databases.

The Emergence of a Solution

Out of the ashes of the first wave of e-commerce experimentation, a new technology architecture is emerging. This technology architecture, known as a Web services architecture, responds to major challenges that previous generations of technology have been unable to address. Despite its name, the focus of a Web services architecture is not to connect people with Web sites. Instead, it focuses on connecting applications and data directly with each other, automating connections that might otherwise have required human intervention. The architecture is designed to ensure that applications and data can be accessed by authorized entities, regardless of location or underlying technology platforms.

The key innovation of this new architecture is to loosely couple resources so that they can be dynamically accessed across multiple entities and diverse technology platforms. Loose coupling means that the connections can be established without being tailored to the specific functionality embedded in the applications to be connected. The loose coupling is in stark contrast to existing enterprise architectures in which the tight coupling of resources became the primary means for delivering operating efficiencies.

Challenges Addressed

Web services architectures respond to three technological and business challenges:

- *Distributed centers of control.* Connecting applications and data becomes particularly challenging when there is no central decision maker who can impose a common set of technology platforms. Within the enterprise, CIOs may have the authority required to impose common platforms. Even outside the enterprise, a dominant customer or supplier can sometimes impose common platforms on business partners, as occurred in the deployment of EDI networks. Not only can dominant customers or suppliers impose common technology platforms on business partners more readily than fragmented customers or suppliers, dominant customers or suppliers help to establish a richer shared context that increases the potential for successful communication. Unfortunately, as the number of business partners grows and as the range of relationships that each business partner must support expands, the assumptions of a single point of control and context become increasingly untenable.

- *Diversity of technology platforms.* Without a single point of control, businesses must wrestle with a growing diversity of technology platforms that need to be connected. The *n*-squared problem rears its ugly head as the number of connections expands. Equally important, the connections must be feasible for smaller enterprises to establish as well; they must be affordable both in terms of technology investment and in terms of the skills an enterprise needs to operate them.

- *Dynamic environment.* With rapidly changing business conditions, new business partners need to be connected quickly and in a cost-effective manner. What's more, the participants need to retain the flexibility to leave specific business relationships without undue expense or technology investment write-offs.

Architectural Principles

In response to these challenges, four broad principles shape Web services architectures:

- *Simplicity.* Reduce the complexity at the end points of the connections to make it easier and less costly for new participants to establish connections. To the extent that complexity is required for the establishment and management of connections, centralize the complexity and deliver the functionality to all participants as a shared service. Create the functionality once, rather than forcing all participants to replicate the functionality at each end point. As we shall see, simplicity at the end points is the basic inspiration behind the service grid, a key component of a Web services architecture.

- *Loose coupling.* Build a modular architecture in which the interfaces of each module incorporate a limited number of publicly defined standards and protocols to support connections. Design the connections across modules so that they are loosely coupled and, as a result, can be used across a broad range of diverse modules. Loose coupling also makes it easier to quickly establish connections as needed, rather than requiring lengthy lead times. Earlier generations of component-based architectures like CORBA (Common Object Request Broker Architecture) anticipated some of the sensibility of Web services architectures, but they failed to generate ubiquitous standards, in part because the specifications quickly became very complex. Loose coupling also is the key to centralizing complexity through shared services without limiting the flexibility and openness of the underlying network. These shared services are not hard-wired into the network. Instead, they are optional services that can be tailored to meet the needs of individual connections.

- *Heterogeneity.* Honor the diversity of computing platforms and applications that has evolved within and across businesses. Do not assume that businesses will need to shift to a single platform or application set in order to maximize economic value. Focus instead on creating simple overlays that help connect and coordinate these resources so that more economic value can be generated.

- *Openness.* Ensure a solid foundation of ubiquitous standards and protocols to reduce concerns about lock-in and to maximize the participants' return on investment in standards and protocols. Create extensible standards and protocols to maintain simplicity at the outset while preserving the ability to refine the standards and protocols over time to address highly specialized needs. Leverage existing open platforms like the Internet.

FIGURE 2 - 1

Web Services Architecture: An Overview

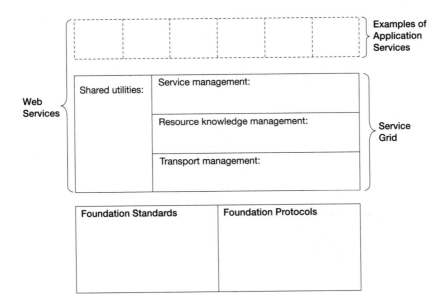

Architectural Components

Web services architectures implement these principles using an emerging set of publicly defined standards and protocols and centralizing much of the complexity of connections in shared service grids. Although much of the media attention has focused on the emerging standards and protocols, discussions often neglect the service grid as a key component of this architecture. The service grid is necessary to harness the potential of the standards and protocols. Figure 2-1 provides an overview of the major components of a Web services architecture.

Foundation Standards and Protocols. Web services architectures are built on a foundation set of standards and protocols (figure 2-2). When people refer to Web services technology, they are generally focusing on this foundation set of standards and protocols. Some of these standards and protocols are reasonably well defined today, whereas others are still in the early stages of definition and will

FIGURE 2 - 2

Web Services Architecture: Standards and Protocols

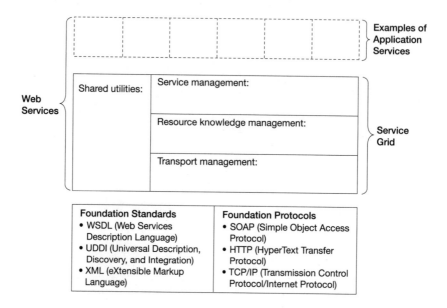

likely evolve substantially as the architecture develops. The most important attribute of all Web services architecture standards and protocols is that they are defined and maintained by broadly supported public standards bodies. This means that they are more likely to be broadly adopted by both technology vendors and users, who do not have to worry about a specific vendor creating lock-in advantage relative to other vendors. From a user perspective, this offers significant advantage in terms of flexibility in picking the best technology vendors without the user having to worry about the ability to connect to other technologies. Users also maximize the return on investment in the implementation of the standards and protocols because the investment can be amortized across a much broader range of applications.

Standards are common formats for representing entities like documents, products, and customers, and actions like "ship" or "confirm." Perhaps the best-known Internet standard is Hypertext Markup Language (HTML), which describes how the graphics and text of a document should be displayed when they are delivered to a user.

HTML is enormously useful when a person is accessing material on a Web site, but it becomes less relevant when computers are accessing information from other computers. For example, a customer's procurement application may want to search a number of supplier electronic catalogs to find out if a product is available in a certain size. Where would it look in order to find size information? XML would address this need.

XML provides a way for "tags" to be created in documents or messages so that other applications can quickly locate the information they need. In the preceding example, the managers of supplier catalogs could implement an XML tag designating where product size information is located. By providing a common format for representing this information, XML makes it easier to automate connections across applications. Where a human had to search for information, the information can now be automatically accessed and delivered.

Another advantage of XML is that it is a standard defined by the broad-based W3C. XML provides much of the same functionality that the formats defined by various EDI vendors in earlier years provided. The key difference is that XML formats are broadly adopted, whereas EDI formats were proprietary to specific vendors. All the major technology vendors, including IBM, Microsoft, Sun Microsystems, BEA, and Oracle, have embraced XML. Even leading application vendors like PeopleSoft and SAP are racing to implement XML standards within their major application suites.

XML also serves as the foundation for other, more specialized standards. For example, Universal Description, Discovery, and Integration (UDDI) is built using XML but is emerging as a more specialized standard to create business registries. As more and more applications become accessible across enterprises in Web services architectures, a key challenge will be to locate the appropriate resource for a specific business need. UDDI addresses this need by establishing a format for organizing directories of resources—think of it as the equivalent of a telephone book, but one that is readable by other computers, rather than by human beings. This standard helps automate the process of searching for appropriate resources.

Another standard, Web Services Description Language (WSDL), addresses a related need. It is a specialized XML format for describing the functionality of applications that can be accessed in a Web services architecture and for providing instructions on how to access the applications electronically. Again, because this format is readable by computers, WSDL helps automate the process of comparing the functionality of specific Web-services-enabled applications and accessing the appropriate applications.

Standards are only part of the solution to establishing automated connections across applications and databases. Protocols are also required in the creation of standardized procedures for establishing and managing connections. Web services architectures start with well-established Internet protocols like Transaction Control Protocol/Internet Protocol (TCP/IP) and HyperText Transfer Protocol (HTTP), which establish rules for communication on the Internet.

Building on top of these protocols, Web services architectures also use a new protocol—Simple Object Access Protocol (SOAP). Like the aforementioned standards, SOAP is built on XML. It is designed to help programs running under different operating systems in electronic networks to communicate with each other. The protocol specifies how to create a message header, or address, and a related XML-based message so that a program in one computer can call a program in another computer and pass it information. SOAP is in the early stages of development and is likely to evolve significantly over time to handle a broader range of communication needs. Because they use HTTP as a foundation protocol, SOAP-enabled messages can more readily cross enterprise firewalls. For this reason, SOAP is particularly valuable for connections across enterprises (although, in the process, the protocol also raises some significant security concerns).

The standards and protocols just discussed will continue to evolve while new standards and protocols will also emerge to address unmet needs. Throughout this process there is a risk that certain vendors will seek to co-opt the standards or protocols and manipulate them for their own proprietary advantage. So far, however, the results have been encouraging. Companies that are otherwise intense rivals have rallied around the early Web services standards. Nevertheless, this is an area that merits close monitoring, which could provide an early warning of potential obstacles to adoption. Executives in leading nontechnology companies need to become strong advocates of open standards and protocols that remain independent of individual technology vendors.

The Service Grid. Standards and protocols are critical to shape the potential of a new Web services architecture. The service grid determines whether that potential gets realized. It is in many respects the critical missing link in the development of a robust technology architecture capable of supporting mission-critical business needs.

The service grid has so far received relatively little attention by proponents of Web services technology and, as a result, is in a relatively early stage of development. For technology providers, it therefore represents a significant business opportunity. For technology users, the grid represents a key measuring standard to determine the state of development of the technology and the range of applications it is truly able to support.

What is the service grid? The service grid consists of a set of specialized utilities providing a broad range of enabling services to both users and providers of applications, as itemized in figure 2-3. These enabling services help make applications more valuable both to users and providers without increasing the complexity for either group. At its broadest level, the service grid performs four roles:

- *Deliver mission-critical functionality.* The most important applications in an enterprise support mission-critical activities like managing supply chains or processing transactions for customers. In these areas, businesses have little tolerance for disruptions. The applications must be available at all times, perform reliably, maintain appropriate security, and deliver results quickly. Although the applications themselves must meet these requirements, it is equally important that the connections across applications also meet these requirements. When these connections are established using Internet technology, concerns immediately arise. The Internet is low-cost and ubiquitous, but it also has performance problems in terms of reliability, security, and speed. Managed

FIGURE 2-3

Web Services Architecture: Service Grid

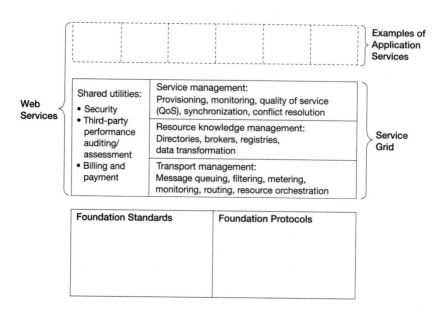

services are necessary for the design and delivery of additional functionality around the connections established across Web services.

- *Create, discover, refine, and disseminate shared meaning.* XML represents a powerful format for the representation of data, but businesses need to agree on shared meaning for specific business terms in order to make XML truly useful. In the example used earlier in the chapter, an XML tag may be helpful in designating where product size information is presented, but do all parties agree on the meaning of product size? Is size represented in inches or centimeters? Does it list height before length and width, or vice versa? Without agreement on specific terms, serious misunderstandings can occur. Businesses will benefit by having specialized utilities and tools to help develop and refine shared meaning using XML formats. Shared meaning cannot be specified fully at the outset—it evolves as misunderstandings and exceptions arise. The misunderstandings and exceptions indicate where shared meaning does not yet exist.

- *Support the capture of monetary value from Web services.* Web services architectures create an opportunity for companies to offer distinctive applications and information as shared services to other companies. This opportunity will only be exploited, however, if there are mechanisms in place to ensure that only authorized users have access, to monitor usage of the shared services, to generate bills for services rendered, and to collect payments.

- *Find and access appropriate resources.* As more and more applications and data become accessible in Web services architectures, businesses will be challenged to find and connect with the most appropriate resources. Many factors, including scalability, reliability, and performance within specific technology environments, will determine appropriateness. Shared managed services exploiting the capabilities of UDDI and WSDL will be necessary to help connect potential users with appropriate resources.

The first two roles of the service grid become critical to accelerating and expanding the early adoption of Web services. Without mission-critical functionality, Web services architectures will play a much more limited role restricted to relatively marginal applications like delivering noncritical information to wireless access devices. Without the development of shared meaning, Web services architectures will evolve more slowly and the pace of adoption will be determined by the ability of businesses to develop shared meaning through other mechanisms. Early efforts to create shared meaning through industry consortia like RosettaNet provide sobering evidence of the challenges ahead. RosettaNet focuses on defining standards for key business processes in the high-tech industry. It set out to define standards for a broad range of partner interface processes (business processes like order management and inventory management), but after several years of effort, RosettaNet has completed work on only a small fraction of them.

The last two roles of the service grid—the capture of monetary value and the attainment of appropriate resources—become more important as adoption becomes more widespread. As later chapters will discuss, the early adoption of Web services architectures will tend to focus on establishing connections across applications of existing business partners. In these cases, the ability to charge for access to applications or data is less critical—the resulting business benefits in terms of operating cost savings and asset savings will provide sufficient motivation for a business to offer access. Since the early adoption will likely involve connections of a few well-established applications across existing business partners, there will be relatively little difficulty in finding and accessing appropriate resources. The challenge will become more severe as the number and variety of applications and other resources grow.

Four broad categories of enabling services will emerge within the service grid to perform the roles just outlined:

- *Service management.* These enabling services help manage applications that are made available in a Web services architecture, ensuring that they meet certain performance specifications and that potential conflicts in usage are effectively resolved.

- *Resource knowledge management.* This layer focuses on enabling services required to help participants in a Web services architecture find each other and communicate effectively with each other.

- *Transport management.* The most basic layer of enabling service, this involves services to increase the reliability of automated message delivery across applications, as well as providing value-added functionality such as the ability to specify complex routing rules for messages to coordinate activities across multiple applications.

- *Shared utilities.* These enabling services are useful not only for application providers but also for other enabling service providers, offering enhanced security capabilities, third-party auditing and assessment of Web service performance, and billing and payment services.

The service grid is a key conceptual component of a Web services architecture. In practice, the functionality delivered by the service grid would be provided by specialized utilities. Even today, we see specialized transport management providers like Grand Central and Flamenco Networks and specialized security service providers like Verisign beginning to offer some of the services just described. Major existing enterprises are getting into the act, like Citibank with CitiConnect, its payment-processing engine, made available to other companies as a Web service. At least in the early stages, these services are likely to be offered by fragmented utility businesses that begin with one set of specialized services. The utility businesses may concentrate within the aforementioned layers, but it is unclear whether there will be even broader concentration across all the functionality required from a service grid.

Unless such broad concentration quickly emerges, we are likely to see other categories of service grid players—the service integrator and the service aggregator. The service integrator would work with individual enterprises to integrate a custom array of specialized utilities to provide the specific service grid functionality required by that enterprise. Service aggregators would package together groups of specialized utilities to provide the functionality required by a broader segment of enterprises, perhaps aggregating one package for the highly fragmented real estate industry and another package for the more concentrated airline industry. Of course, large enterprises might choose to integrate their own custom package of specialized service grid utilities. In this way, we will see many specialized service grids emerge in practice, rather than a single service grid.

All of this functionality could also be provided by software utilities installed within the enterprise. Managers who choose this option, however, must wrestle with significant complexity, both in terms of the implementation of the software and then in terms of the management of regular upgrades of functionality. This complexity is not restricted to one enterprise, since this approach typically requires that all other enterprises seeking to connect install the same software. Just ensuring that everyone has the same release level of the software utilities over time becomes a major challenge. The n-squared problem discussed earlier quickly rears its ugly head.

In practice, we are likely to see federated services emerge, with some of the functionality required for the service grid provided from within enterprises, other elements provided by service aggregators, and yet other elements provided by stand-alone enabling service providers. The specific form of federation will be tailored and will evolve based on the application or user needs.

By centralizing this functionality and delivering it as an enabling service rather than as software installed within the enterprise, the service grid reduces the complexity that each participating enterprise must support. In effect, it solves the n-squared problem by making it a much simpler "$2n$" problem. In other words, rather than forcing each participant in the architecture to implement tailored connections to every other participant, the service grid only requires each participant to implement one simple interface and then helps to facilitate connections to any other participant. The service grid does more than reduce complexity for participants. It also creates a concentration point to attract, retain, and develop the highly specialized skills required to create, deliver, and refine these enabling services. In this respect, the service grid transforms the n-squared problem into an attractive feature. By providing an opportunity for enabling service providers to interact with a growing range of participants, the service grid creates an opportunity for accelerated learning and rapid performance improvement.

Take the example of security services. These services require highly specialized expertise that, in the absence of a service grid, would need to be dispersed across each enterprise. Even very large enterprises would have difficulty building the depth necessary to ensure world-class security capability. Since security is not the primary focus of these enterprises, their security experts would always be second-class citizens within the organization. As a result, attracting and retaining the best would be a major challenge. In contrast, companies specializing in providing security services as part of the service grid would provide a more compelling development opportunity for security experts. In part, this is because specialized security service companies would be well positioned to learn from security experiences across a broad range of customers and could use this learning to continually refine their service offering and deepen the expertise of their employees. Although all enterprises would need to retain some security expertise within

FIGURE 2 - 4

Web Services Architecture: Application Services

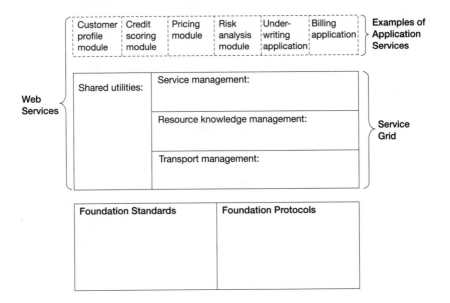

their company, they would benefit by relying on more specialized providers for broad elements of their security program.

Application Services. Application services represent the third broad component of a Web services architecture (figure 2-4). In contrast to enabling services, application services provide functionality targeted to specific end-user business activities like loan processing, human resource management, or logistics planning. Designed to support broad classes of applications, enabling services tend to have a much broader range of use. The term *Web services* includes both enabling services and application services.

Application services can take many forms. In the early stages, they may start as conventional applications, like inventory management or order entry, that have been "exposed" and can be accessed as part of a Web services architecture.

The process of exposing an existing application involves the development of a new interface to the application. This application

interface converts data and functionality into appropriate XML formats, creates appropriate descriptions of the application service,
and implements the SOAP protocols necessary to manage connections with other applications. The effort required to develop this
interface can vary significantly, depending on how the underlying
application is structured and documented, but it is generally modest. Leading application service providers (IBM, Microsoft, BEA, Sun
Microsystems, and Oracle) and more focused start-ups (Cape Clear,
Interkeel, and Killdara) are now making substantial investments in
software tools and utilities to automate the process for implementing these new interfaces. The result is even simpler and lower-cost
interfaces. Over time, more applications will be developed with interfaces using Web services standards and protocols from the start.

Application services can cover a broad spectrum in terms of
functionality. When the media focus on application services, they
use examples of relatively simple, stand-alone microservices like a
currency calculator that can be accessed by cell phones. These are
relatively modest applications, but they acquire more business value
if they connect into broader applications like enterprise procurement. At an even higher level of functionality, the entire procurement application could be made available as an application service, perhaps connecting into a broader supply-chain-management
application. Moving further along the functionality spectrum, an
application service might actually become the front end for a business service like outsourced manufacturing operations or call-center
operations, helping the outsourcer better coordinate activities with
the outsourcing provider, wherever its operations are located.

As we will see in chapter 3, an early wave of application service
providers created significant confusion relative to the potential of
Web services architectures. With a few exceptions, these early application service providers were simply taking very traditional enterprise applications and delivering them on a shared basis from outside
the enterprise firewall. They used few if any of the aforementioned
elements of a Web services architecture to connect these shared
applications with applications within the enterprise.

The publicity garnered by this first wave of application service
providers led many to believe that application service providers
would naturally be specialized third-party companies developing

and delivering application services as their core business. Instead, as a later chapter will discuss, Web services architectures have been adopted first by enterprises seeking to connect their existing applications with the applications of their business partners. In effect, traditional enterprises have become the first ASPs. A new generation of specialized ASPs will certainly emerge, but it will take time for them to do so and to gain acceptance.

Obstacles along the Way

Web services technology offers significant potential to address unmet business needs for enhanced flexibility and collaboration. Given the early stage of the technology, it is important to stress the word "potential." Business managers need to be aware that there is no guarantee that this potential will be realized. There are many obstacles along the way. By understanding these obstacles and monitoring progress in addressing them, managers can make better decisions regarding the deployment of this technology.

The three most significant obstacles have been discussed earlier in this chapter:

- *Fragmentation of standards and protocols.* The power of Web services technology lies in the ubiquitous adoption of its core standards and protocols. As these standards and protocols evolve, there is a continuing risk that vendors will seek to introduce proprietary versions, reducing the interoperability of the technology.

- *Limited availability of enabling services in the service grid.* A rich set of enabling services in the service grid will need to be available to businesses to ensure rapid and broad adoption within mission-critical business activities. The service grid is truly the "missing link" in Web services architectures today. If established companies or entrepreneurial start-ups move slowly to provide the necessary enabling services, companies considering the adoption of this technology will be much more reluctant to make broad commitments.

- *Challenges in establishing shared meaning.* If shared meaning does not evolve quickly or remains narrowly confined to

small groups of business partners, it will be much more difficult to realize the potential of the technology for business
collaboration. We could witness the same Balkanization of
business activity that has occurred in the EDI realm. The
speed and breadth of evolution of shared meaning hinges
much more on business issues like competitive dynamics
and trust than on purely technological issues such as the
availability of tools.

Business executives need to do more than monitor progress in
addressing each of these obstacles. Through their actions, they can
have a significant impact on efforts to overcome them. If business
executives become aggressive evangelists and advocates for ubiquitous standards, for the development of appropriate enabling services, and for initiatives to accelerate and broaden development
of shared meaning, these efforts are much more likely to succeed.
If business executives remain silent, these obstacles will become
much more formidable. The risk will increase substantially that
Web services technology will never realize its full potential.

The bottom line is that the potential of Web services technology is far from assured. Significant effort will be required to ensure
that the obstacles currently confronting the technology are successfully overcome. While executives of technology companies can
make a major difference in the likelihood of success, business executives more broadly cannot afford to defer to technology companies. Business executives must play an active role in shaping the
evolution of this technology.

Where Is the Real Power?

Web services architectures are like a Rorschach test for technologists. Depending on their background and interests, technologists
will highlight different dimensions of this architecture. From a
business perspective focusing on where economic value will be created in the near term, a very different element of the architecture
becomes relevant.

Some technologists will highlight the movement from application to service as the key differentiation of the architecture. With

conventional applications, a business actually needs to install the software within the enterprise or implement expensive connections to provide access across networks. For application services, the actual physical location of the underlying application becomes irrelevant. As long as the application service is exposed within a Web services architecture, authorized users, regardless of location or the underlying technology platforms, can access it.

Other technologists will focus on the dimension of components as the distinctive feature. For decades, software designers have sought to create modular approaches to software development that would allow modules to be reused and thereby enhance the designers' productivity. By defining a standardized set of interfaces for applications, Web services architectures are certainly part of the broader class of modular approaches to software development. The distinctive feature of Web services architectures is that the standards used to create common interfaces for applications are based on the ubiquitous XML standard. Previous approaches to modular design tended to employ more narrowly adopted standards that limited the potential value of the approach.

Web services architectures represent an interesting fusion of these two dimensions—services and components. We are seeing the emergence of a new kind of distributed service architecture in which common interfaces convert applications into service modules that can be accessed from anywhere at any time. Designers may eventually even compose new, dynamic applications that are tailored to the need of the moment and that automatically access the appropriate application services and connect them, providing exactly the right functionality at the right time.

We are a long way from realizing such visions. As later chapters discuss, these capabilities can provide the basis for some very powerful, new approaches to business growth over time. But what will drive the early implementation of Web services architectures is much simpler. It is the ability to quickly establish flexible connections across existing applications at much lower cost than has been possible with previous generations of technology. By offering business managers this capability, Web services architectures create an opportunity to deliver significant operating cost and asset savings for the enterprise. For business managers, the truly distinctive attribute of this architecture in the near term is its ability to establish much more flexible connections in business operations, especially in operations that span several enterprises.

As chapter 1 suggested, managers need to deliver continuing rounds of operating cost and asset savings while at the same time accelerating growth. To do this they must escape from the high cost and inflexible infrastructures that make both cost reduction and growth so challenging. Web services architectures provide business managers with both the flexibility and the collaboration capability required to meet the challenge of ambitious operating savings and growth objectives.

3

A False Start

Application Service Providers

THE FIREWALL is a key component of existing enterprise architectures. Designed to prevent unwanted intruders from accessing enterprise resources, a firewall also makes it difficult for the enterprise to access outside resources to leverage its own operations.

Application service providers (ASPs) represented the first wave to move beyond the firewall. These companies largely took traditional enterprise applications like supply-chain management and human resource management and moved them outside the firewall in an effort to serve small and medium-sized enterprises. ASPs garnered a lot of publicity when the first wave launched. On the surface, many attributes of ASPs were very appealing. Unfortunately, significant challenges lurked beneath the surface.

ASPs in many respects represented a false start in the efforts to break out of the enterprise straitjacket. In particular, few of them adopted Web services architectures as their technology platform. Instead, they attempted to build businesses on the Internet using traditional technology architectures. As we will see, this proved to be a significant flaw in the early ASP model and explains many difficulties these businesses experienced.

Nevertheless, we can learn much by understanding the limitations of this first wave of ASPs. These lessons provide the beginning of a road map for those now working to breach the walls of the enterprise silo. Readers who understand the distinction between

ASPs and Web services and, in particular, the limitations of the technology platforms of the ASPs may choose to skip this chapter and move on to chapter 4. Others will find it helpful to understand the challenges encountered by ASPs and the implications for their efforts to deliver software more widely as services.

Early ASP Pioneers

Enterprise application vendors like SAP and PeopleSoft initially focused their sales efforts on large enterprises. They met with great success in this arena, but they were far less successful in their efforts to expand into small and medium-sized enterprises. Many economic challenges stood in the way. These enterprises could not afford the large, up-front license fees required by enterprise application vendors. Nor was it cost-effective for a direct sales force to access these smaller enterprises.

As businesses began to see the Internet as a potential platform for commercial activity, a number of entrepreneurs perceived an opportunity to use the Internet to reach small and medium-sized enterprises in a more cost-effective way. These entrepreneurs formed many Internet-based companies focused on delivering enterprise applications to small and medium-sized enterprises.

Collectively, this group of companies became known as application service providers. Table 3-1 shows the various categories of ASPs, with their corresponding major activity. Although the label focuses attention on applications, many of the companies did not provide applications themselves. Instead, they provided the complementary services required to support the delivery of the applications to businesses. In fact, an entire business ecology emerged, with companies playing many different roles in delivering and supporting enterprise applications through the Internet.

If not all of these companies provided applications, what did they have in common? They were all focused on the opportunity to deliver applications from centralized servers as a service, rather than as a product installed on the premises of the customer. The customer could access these applications from the Internet through a conventional Web browser. Delivering applications as a service in turn created an opportunity for a variety of specialized services,

TABLE 3 - 1

Taxonomy of Application Service Providers

Category	Activity
ASP Resellers	Provide new Internet-based distribution channel and "rental" pricing model for traditional enterprise applications
ASP Developers	Develop new applications and deliver on the Internet with "rental" pricing model
ASP Aggregators	Integrate and market packages of applications provided by ASP developers
Hosting Services	Provide specialized facilities and support services for companies deploying Internet-based applications
Managed Services Providers	Provide specialized application management services

such as provision of specialized computer hardware and network facilities and enabling services like security and billing.

During 1999 and the first quarter of 2000, investors poured $3.6 billion into various ASP businesses. More than two thousand companies were claiming the ASP mantle. IDC (International Data Corporation) estimated that ASPs in the United States collectively generated $547 million in revenue in 2000, an impressive number for such an early stage of development, but less remarkable if spread over two thousand companies. Let's review the various categories of companies that emerged under the ASP umbrella.

ASP Resellers

ASP resellers like Corio, Applicast, and USinternetworking, founded in 1998, received the most media attention. Serving as resellers, these companies saw an opportunity to source enterprise applications from established vendors. They focused on developing a new Internet-based distribution channel to deliver and support these applications more economically for small and medium-sized enterprises.

A novel approach to pricing represented a key part of the resellers' value proposition. Rather than requiring customers to "purchase" an expensive software license in order to use the application software, ASP resellers would instead "rent" access to the application, charging much lower usage fees on a monthly basis. (Service bureaus in the 1970s actually were the first to pioneer this pricing approach. These service bureaus in many respects represented an early version of the ASP business model.) Although pricing models varied, they generally incorporated provisions for increasing rental fees based on a variety of usage metrics (for example, increasing charges as the number of users grew or as the number of interactions with the applications expanded). In many cases, customers might pay as much over time for access to the applications under the ASP model as they would under more traditional licensing models. The key difference, though, was that ASPs sharply reduced the initial payment required for a customer to gain access to applications and "back-loaded" payments based on actual usage. For CFOs concerned about the timing of cash outlays, the ASP pricing model appeared attractive.

ASP Developers

A smaller group of companies saw an opportunity to develop new applications and to use the Internet as the channel to reach potential customers. Companies like Employease, Salesforce.com, and NetLedger led in this category. Employease was founded in 1996, earlier than the ASP resellers, but most of the ASP developers emerged in 1998 and later.

The more ambitious companies targeted some of the same application categories as the enterprise application vendors did. Employease focused on human resource management applications, Salesforce.com targeted customer relationship applications, and NetLedger went after basic accounting applications. Another group of ASP developers concentrated on much more limited applications like expense reporting (Captura), printing and mailing services (Eletter), and Web conferencing services (PlaceWare).

In many respects, ASP developers focusing on traditional enterprise application categories faced much greater challenges than did ASP resellers. The resellers had ready-made applications and could go to market quickly, leveraging the installed base of reference customers already developed by their enterprise application vendor partners. ASP developers had to invest more money up front and had to endure longer lead times to get to market since they needed to first develop the application. Since their products were at an earlier stage of commercialization, the applications often did not have as rich a feature set as those of the more established enterprise software vendors, and the ASP developers certainly did not have the luxury of an installed base that could be referenced.

To compensate, ASP developers did have one significant advantage. They did not have to rely on the client server architecture that had been the foundation for all the major enterprise application vendors. This client server architecture was not well suited for delivery over the Internet. It assumed that much of the application logic would need to reside in a "fat" client, typically a PC on the desktop of the application user. This approach was originally designed for local area networks within an enterprise. It worked much less effectively over the Internet because a substantial amount of data had to be continuously exchanged between the client and the server for the application to work. A reasonable degree of reliability and performance under this architecture required considerable bandwidth in the network connections. At a minimum, such an architecture usually imposed a significant performance overhead on the Internet and reliability often suffered as well.

Recognizing these limitations, ASP developers learned from the early experience of Internet applications. They employed a very different technology approach that concentrated most of the application activity at the server level, thus reducing significantly the need to exchange data between the client and the server. In this respect, the applications were optimized for use over the Internet.

In addition, at least some ASP developers used object-oriented programming techniques. These techniques, not widely available in traditional enterprise applications, made it much easier to develop applications as modules that could be plugged together on an as-needed basis. With this modular approach, ASP developers found it much easier and more cost-effective to tailor applications to the needs of particular customers. The lack of a modular approach in traditional enterprise applications explains the substantial investments customers had to make in order to customize applications for the needs of their particular businesses. The modular approach also made it easier for some ASP developers to compete on functionality with ASP resellers and their enterprise application vendor partners. Their applications may not have matched the functionality of more established vendors at the outset, but the modular architecture employed by ASP developers allowed them to more rapidly enhance their products at lower cost.

ASP Aggregators

In response to the emergence of ASP developers, another category of company emerged. ASP aggregators sought to take the specialized applications offered by many ASP developers, knit them together into a single interoperable package, and market them to business customers. Jamcracker and Agiliti, both founded in 1999, were perhaps the two most prominent examples of this category of business. They hired direct sales forces, created sophisticated integration platforms, and negotiated partnerships with a range of ASP developers.

Hosting Services

Hosting services had already begun to emerge in the mid-1990s, focused on providing specialized facilities and support services for companies seeking to deploy Internet-based applications. Many companies were wrestling with the complexities of deploying and managing sophisticated Internet-based technology platforms. Whether they were traditional enterprises creating Web sites for customers and partners, ASP developers, or new Internet-based companies, few had the internal capability to deploy and manage the technology required to be successful. These companies still had to hire dedicated operations staff, procure the technology platforms and data center facilities required for their applications, create a secure operating environment, and manage reliable operations that were increasingly becoming mission-critical.

Hosting companies like Exodus, UUNet (part of WorldCom), and Verio (affiliated with NTT) recognized that companies focused on the Internet were seeking to leverage their operations. Dot-coms, companies using the Internet exclusively as a business platform, were concentrating on sustaining extraordinary growth rates through aggressive customer acquisition. They welcomed the

chance to outsource the operation of their Internet technology platforms to specialized providers. Bricks-and-mortar companies faced a
different challenge. They had limited skills in Internet-based technologies and sought out specialized hosting services to accelerate
entry into market and fill the skill gap within their own companies.

Many ASP resellers and developers relied on hosting services so
that they could concentrate on sales and marketing efforts. ASPs
soon discovered that reaching small and medium-sized enterprises,
convincing them to adopt enterprise applications, and implementing the applications required significant effort. They welcomed any
leverage they could find in terms of operating the technology platforms themselves. Corio, for example, outsourced its data center
operations to Exodus, whereas Agilera, another prominent ASP
reseller, relied on Verio for hosting services.

Managed Service Providers

Another group of companies saw a different opportunity. Hosting
services, at least at the outset, were often stripped-down providers
of data center facilities. Even as these hosting services developed a
broader range of value-added management services, they often
continued to focus on facility management, rather than application management.

This created an opportunity for a new class of company, known
as managed service providers (MSPs). These companies specialized
in managing the operation of the applications themselves, and
often outsourced the ownership and management of the capital-
intensive data center facilities to hosting services. Loudcloud,
founded by Marc Andreessen, one of the high-profile founders of
Netscape, was perhaps the best known MSP. Founded in 1999,
Loudcloud was quickly joined by many other players, including
SiteSmith, Nuclio, and Digex.

The ASP Promise

When ASPs entered the market, they garnered significant media
attention. The ASP promise appeared compelling at the time. In
many respects, ASPs seemed to be logical extensions of a much

broader outsourcing trend. At a time when companies were looking for speed, flexibility, asset leverage, and access to world-class capabilities, ASPs appeared to offer a winning business model.

Capability Leverage

Like all outsourcing businesses, ASPs offered the promise of access to world-class capabilities from specialized providers, rather than an enterprise's having to develop them internally. To begin with, ASPs offered small and medium-sized enterprises the opportunity to access sophisticated enterprise applications that, because of high up-front licensing fees, had previously not been available to them. ASPs or their business partners also provided access to skilled technology staff to manage the operation and maintenance of the applications. At a time when an industry group estimated that 850,000 information technology jobs were going unfilled, access to skilled staff proved very attractive. Customers also gained access to specialized facilities and computer hardware to run the applications.

Economic Leverage

For companies concerned about cash, ASPs appeared to offer clear benefits as well. Many ASPs claimed to reduce substantially the total cost of ownership of enterprise applications by providing customers access to large-scale and highly specialized (and therefore presumably lower-cost) operations and facilities. Industry analysts estimated that the total cost of ownership of applications could be reduced by as much as 30 to 50 percent through the use of ASPs, although these claims were controversial.

Even if the total cost of ownership was not substantially reduced, ASPs offered attractive cash-flow advantages. Large up-front payments for software licenses, computer hardware, operating facilities, and dedicated technical staff were substantially reduced in favor of periodic payments that varied with usage. If the applications were heavily used, the customer might actually end up paying more under an ASP pricing scheme, but the payments would be spread out over time and much more tightly linked to usage and, hopefully, business benefit. Just looking at the cost of the application itself as an example, large enterprises often paid as much as $250,000 for a license to install a customer relationship management (CRM) application from SAP or Oracle, whereas small enterprises could access CRM applications for as little as $50 per month.

The ability to reduce the risk of technology obsolescence also lured customers. Customers were vulnerable to rapid technology innovation if they bought traditional enterprise applications and installed them in their companies. Customers would face very high switching costs if they attempted to take advantage of a new enterprise application with superior functionality. In contrast, if the customers were simply "renting" their applications and the associated specialized facilities and staff, they potentially faced lower switching costs. More sophisticated customers realized that the bulk of the switching costs in moving from one application to another was not in the technology itself, but rather in the changes required in business operations to adapt to the demands of a new application. Nevertheless, customers could at least avoid technology obsolescence in the underlying technology platforms (e.g., servers, network facilities, and software utilities) by sourcing their applications through ASPs.

Speed and Flexibility

When ASPs first emerged, perhaps the most compelling promise they offered was increased speed and flexibility. At a time when "Speed is God" had become the mantra, anything that promised to reduce lead times had great appeal. Similarly, when Internet-based businesses appeared to be seriously challenging more traditional companies and well-accepted rules of business seemed no longer to hold true, anything that promised to increase flexibility was guaranteed to get an audience.

Since customers could forgo the time-consuming tasks of hiring specialized operations staff, preparing facilities, and installing complex application software on their premises, ASPs appeared to be able to substantially reduce the extensive lead times involved in implementing enterprise applications. One estimate suggested that implementation lead times could be reduced from as much as several years to as little as a few months. USinternetworking, for example, boasted average implementation cycles of seventy-five days.

New releases of enterprise applications offered customers the opportunity to access new features and capabilities. Yet, the expense and lead time required for the installation of a new release of an enterprise application represented a significant dilemma to customers. They wanted access to the most up-to-date functionality, but dreaded the burden imposed by frequent upgrades. ASPs appeared to address this dilemma by greatly simplifying the upgrade process. Much of the upgrade activity was concentrated in the facility of the ASP, making it lower cost and faster for the customer to implement upgrades. ASPs created the expectation that, as the cost and speed of upgrades improved, application developers would compress their upgrade cycles, giving customers access to the most up-to-date functionality possible.

The ASP Reality

In reality, the ASP promise proved far less compelling to customers than originally expected. Unfortunately for the customer, most companies in the first wave of ASPs were simply repurposed software providers (RSPs). They were not leveraging new technologies to create better applications. Instead, they were tightly linked to traditional enterprise architectures. They were really only moving traditional enterprise architectures outside the enterprise firewall and offering them on a rental basis rather than on a more conventional license-fee basis. As a result, RSPs offered little distinctive value in terms of features and actually created additional performance concerns. This reality led to a significant gap between promise and performance. Issues regarding the applications and their delivery overshadowed any underlying economic benefits.

Product Complexity and Lack of Flexibility

Founders of the first wave of ASPs were driven by one key assumption: Small and medium-sized enterprises would benefit by accessing the capabilities offered by traditional enterprise applications. This assumption proved questionable on two levels.

First, traditional enterprise applications were designed to meet the complex needs of a large enterprise. Small and medium-sized enterprises rarely needed the full complex functionality embedded in these applications. As a result, the applications proved unwieldy in smaller enterprises—they were slower and more complicated than necessary. Rather than being superior to existing applications targeted to small and medium-sized enterprises, these enterprise applications often were viewed as inferior in terms of fit with the needs of the business.

Second, many benefits associated with the remote delivery of these applications proved illusory. Applications designed using conventional technology architectures presented major challenges when businesses tried to customize them or to connect them with their existing applications. The expense and lead times associated with the implementation of traditional enterprise applications did not stem from the need to install these applications on the premises. Instead, the expense and lead times were much more related to the need to customize applications or to connect to existing applications.

According to the Meta Group, companies on average typically sought to customize at least 10 percent of the functionality in an enterprise application. Customizing a mere 10 percent of the functionality of an enterprise application could increase support expenses by as much as 2 to 3 times over a three-year period.

Remote delivery did nothing to address this issue. In fact, the complexity and expense of trying to connect with existing applications tended to grow exponentially in a remote-delivery environment using traditional technology approaches. As a result, the anticipated cost savings associated with large-scale, specialized operating platforms failed to materialize. In some cases, costs per customer actually escalated as the number of customers increased.

Customers were also disappointed in the expectation of compressed upgrade cycles. The ASP resellers were dependent on the companies developing the enterprise applications. These software companies continued to operate on longer upgrade cycles because most of their customers were still using application software installed on their premises. The ASP developers had more capability to compress upgrade cycles, but the challenging economics of their businesses led them to divert resources from application development to customer acquisition. ASP developers using traditional technologies also found that enhancements to their applications often caused unanticipated performance issues with the links to the established applications of their customers. As a result, they found that upgrades were much more time-consuming and expensive to implement than expected.

Product Performance Concerns

In the absence of distinctive and compelling product differentiation, customers began to focus on concerns about the delivery of, and support for, their applications. CIOs were instinctively resistant to becoming dependent on applications that operated outside their firewall. Within the firewall, they had much better control over performance. Outside the firewall, they worried about both technical and corporate performance.

In terms of technology, ASPs delivered the applications across the public Internet. CIOs were concerned about security—could third parties gain access to confidential corporate information? Reliability and availability were also concerns. Mission-critical business applications in sensitive areas like supply-chain management required reliable connections at all times. Even a few hours of downtime could result in disruptions to manufacturing operations. ASPs offered service-level agreements to commit explicitly to certain levels of performance, but the agreements did not eliminate the perceived risk. They only offered contractual remedies for companies damaged by performance shortfalls. Service-level agreements thus offered little consolation for risk-averse CIOs, who realized that their jobs might well be on the line if the ASPs failed to perform.

Vendor Performance Concerns

On the vendor side, CIOs also had concerns. ASPs were new start-ups, often with a very limited track record. Technology could certainly be a factor in performance, but defective management processes could also create performance problems. CIOs found that ASPs had very limited operating history to provide reassurance that their management processes had been tested successfully in high-volume, mission-critical environments.

Even if CIOs could get comfortable about the management processes of the ASP, they confronted another risk. What happened if the ASP did not succeed as a business? Would the CIOs be left high and dry with applications in the possession of a bankrupt company? Would they even have any warning of an impending bankruptcy? As the next section of this chapter suggests, these concerns about the viability of the ASPs proved well founded.

Challenging Vendor Economics

Originally viewed as the hot new wave of Internet business, ASPs soon found themselves caught in a potentially life-threatening economic bind. Customer concerns about ASP performance and the lack of compelling product benefits contributed to much higher customer acquisition costs than anticipated. Sales cycles were also longer than anticipated, averaging at least three or four months for ASP resellers. Revenue took even longer to materialize, as customers spent more time on pilots to overcome performance concerns. ASPs often resorted to price concessions to encourage trial. The bottom line? It cost more and took longer to acquire customers, and those customers generated less revenue over longer periods. For example, USinternetworking spent $17.7 million on sales and marketing in the second quarter of 2000, which represented about two-thirds of the revenue generated during the same period.

But that's not all. Since there were fewer customers than anticipated, ASPs had a difficult time realizing the scale economics that were so critical to their business. In a high-fixed-cost business, shortfalls in the number of customers can have dramatic impact on profitability. Not only were scale economies failing to materialize, but also operating costs were proving higher than expected because of the cost and complexity of customizing ASP applications and connecting them with the legacy applications of their customers. What the first wave of ASPs failed to appreciate was that license fees represented only one-fifth of the cost of the enterprise application for the customer—fully four-fifths of the cost involved the time- and resource-consuming efforts to implement these applications.

Lower revenue and higher costs—this is not a formula for economic success. It is not surprising, therefore, that the first wave of ASPs confronted serious economic challenges. None were profitable, even after several years of operation. Worse still, the growing awareness of the challenging economics of ASPs reinforced the concerns of potential customers regarding the viability of ASP providers. It made many customers even more reluctant to entrust their key application platforms to potentially unstable third parties.

These economic difficulties reflected an even more fundamental issue. ASPs offered appealing economics to their customers, but in the process, they made their own economics more challenging. ASPs had to pay for their applications and all the technical infrastructure and operating staff up front, but could only cover these expenditures through much smaller monthly charges spread out over several years. Customization and integration needs at the outset gave rise to a very labor-intensive implementation process. ASPs tried to recover some of these expenses through implementation charges, but the need to attract new customers more rapidly led most ASPs to keep these charges low. Although the ASPs needed rapid growth to benefit from scale economics, the requirement of substantial up-front expenditures to serve each new customer meant that high growth undermined near-term profitability.

ASPs are responding aggressively to improve their economics. Many have shifted their customer focus from small and medium-sized enterprises to large enterprises. Large enterprises are more appropriate customers for the enterprise applications offered by the large ASP resellers. These large customers also can generate more revenue, once the ASP establishes the customer relationship. Some ASPs have significantly narrowed their application focus, offering fewer core applications rather than a broad suite. ASPs are also beginning to develop deeper partnerships with third parties like systems integrators and value-added resellers to generate leads and to offload much of the initial implementation expense incurred when new customers are added. Similarly, a growing number of ASP resellers and ASP developers are outsourcing data center operations to specialized hosting services and managed service providers. In this way, ASPs can convert significant portions of their fixed cost structures into variable costs that are incurred only when customers are added.

TABLE 3 - 2

Application Service Providers: Promise versus Reality

ASP Promise	ASP Reality
Capability leverage	Product complexity/lack of flexibility
Economic leverage	Product performance concerns: security, reliability, and availability
Speed and flexibility	Vendor performance concerns: scalability and survival
	Challenging vendor economics

Nevertheless, the first wave of ASPs will continue to face major difficulties in an environment shaped by deteriorating economic circumstances and substantial overcapacity. Table 3-2 summarizes the contrast between what ASPs promised and what they could deliver. The broad-based decline in technology spending that began in early 2000 continued to deepen into 2001. Terrorist attacks in September 2001 sharply increased concerns about security and control of application platforms. As customer demand receded, additional financing sources were also drying up. The proliferation of ASP businesses that occurred in late 1999 and early 2000 will inevitably be followed by significant consolidation. Only the very strongest players have any chance of surviving. In December 2000, industry analysts were predicting that 60 percent of the ASPs in business then would either be acquired or shut down during the following twelve months. Bankruptcy filings by such prominent players as USinternetworking, Applicast, Breakaway Solutions, and Exodus, as well as layoffs by virtually all of the major ASP providers, highlight the challenges ahead.

Lessons Learned from the First Wave of ASPs

The first wave of ASPs attracted considerable attention by promising substantial value in the form of capability and economic leverage, as well as speed and flexibility. The promises were compelling—the ability to deliver on the promise was where the problems arose. By examining the experiences of the first wave of ASPs and the source of the problems they encountered, business

TABLE 3 - 3

Comparison of Software Providers

	Traditional Application Software Providers	Application Service Providers	Web Services Providers
Location of Software	Installed in enterprise	Installed in central facility, delivered remotely to enterprise	Installed anywhere— enterprise, business partners, central facility
Pricing	License fee	Subscription fee	Subscription fee
Ability to Tailor to Individual Customer	Limited	Limited	High
Ability to Enhance over Time	Limited	Limited	High
Difficulty/Cost of Connecting to Diverse Applications	High	High	Low

managers can learn from the mistakes made in this first wave and find new, more sustainable ways to deliver leverage, speed, and flexibility. Four broad lessons emerge from this review of the first wave of ASPs. Web services technology will play a key role in addressing many of the challenges encountered by this wave. Table 3-3 summarizes the differences between three broad providers of software—traditional application software providers, ASPs, and a new generation of Web services providers.

Leverage Is Essential but Not Sufficient

As competition intensifies, businesses need to find ways to more effectively leverage the resources of others, as well as improve speed and flexibility. The attention garnered by ASPs testifies to the power of the unmet business needs they sought to serve. Companies wanted to believe that ASPs could deliver on the promises they made.

But leverage, speed, and flexibility are clearly not sufficient, particularly when an application needs to address mission-critical business activities. Companies must be assured that they will be able to trust the applications supporting their most important business activities. Trust comes in many forms. At one level, it is trust in the applications themselves—trust that they are accessible when needed, reliable in terms of performing predictably, and secure from access by unauthorized parties. At another level, it is trust in the application provider—confidence that the provider will perform as represented, will not abuse the relationship with the customer, and will continue as a viable business.

In both cases, the first wave of ASPs fell short. Most applications were developed from previous generations of technology that were not optimized for use over public networks like the Internet. By using technology that was not ideal for distribution and sharing over wide-area networks, the companies themselves ran into significant economic challenges that threatened their viability.

Web services architectures can significantly help address these additional needs. Web services architectures are optimized for the Internet and, as a result, do not carry the same performance overhead that other technology architectures incur on the Internet. By creating platforms that can be more easily integrated with other providers, Web services architectures encourage specialization. As a result, they are spawning service grids consisting of highly specialized enabling service providers focused in such areas as security, reliable messaging, and monitoring of service performance. The capabilities of these service grids will go a long way in addressing customer concerns and building trust.

Customization and Integration Are Key

The first wave of ASPs encountered perhaps the greatest economic challenges in customizing and integrating the applications they provided. These difficulties stemmed from the hardwired nature of the applications the providers were either reselling or had developed themselves. Using previous generations of technology, ASPs found that even minor changes in the functionality of the application required enormous effort to customize the platform. Integrating these applications into a portfolio of legacy applications created similar challenges because of the need to manage the complexity of a wide range of proprietary interfaces.

Customers will need more customization and integration over time, not less. Competitive pressures are forcing companies not only to develop distinctive approaches to the market, but also to customize those approaches to the needs of individual customers. Similarly, companies are now confronting the need to integrate their business processes well beyond their own enterprise to include the activities of their business partners and customers.

If ASPs are to become a viable business model, they need to adopt a different technology architecture for their applications, one that offers much stronger customization and integration capabilities. Those few ASP developers that embraced component-based architectures have fared much better than most other ASP resellers and ASP developers, in large part because of their ability to automate the customization and integration processes.

Business Focus Enhances Viability

The first wave of ASPs generally tried to do too much, especially in their early days. On reflection, this is understandable given the abundance of financing available and the desire to extend control in an emerging business with great uncertainty. Nevertheless, such an approach increased the amount and range of resources required for success. It also forced ASPs to try to become world-class in a broad set of business activities. Ultimately, it had the perverse effect of increasing risk, rather than reducing risk.

ASP resellers were spread across three very different businesses. They invested heavily to create strong marketing and sales capability, they needed depth in their professional services capability to support the implementation of their applications, and they built a substantial infrastructure to manage the operations of the applications and related technology infrastructure. ASP developers raised the ante even further by seeking to develop their own applications.

Although a broader ecology of businesses emerged to support ASP resellers and ASP developers, as described earlier in the chapter, ASP resellers and developers were often reluctant to leverage their own operations through relationships with these complementary businesses. As the economic slowdown took hold in 2000 to 2001, we have seen a tendency to tighten business focus along multiple business dimensions. In particular, ASPs are responding to growing economic pressure by making difficult choices about what business they are in. At the highest level, they are choosing to focus either on building strong customer relationships as a distribution channel with deep professional services capabilities, or on developing world-class applications, or on offering high-performance management services. These diverse directions map well to the unbundling patterns described later in the book.

Although the mind-set of management caused much of the reluctance to focus in the first wave of ASP deployment, technology also emerged as an obstacle. Previous generations of technology made it difficult to coordinate business activities across dispersed entities on electronic networks. Web services architectures are specifically designed to support this kind of integration. As a result, they should help businesses overcome many of the perceived risks in relying on more specialized providers.

As these architectures become more widely deployed, enterprise users should become increasingly skeptical of ASP claims that they can do it all themselves. The irony is that although the first wave of ASPs were very articulate about the need for their customers to outsource key elements of their business, the ASPs themselves were often reluctant to reap the same benefits of outsourcing.

Application Functionality Needs to Rapidly Evolve

Rapid enhancement of application functionality was one of the early promises made by the first wave of ASPs, but it was soon dropped as the providers confronted the economic realities of their struggling businesses. In addition to the demand for resources in other parts of the business (particularly customer acquisition), ASPs discovered that traditional technology architectures were ill suited to rapid enhancement cycles. Enhancements often had unforeseen consequences in distant areas of massively hardwired applications. Even intensive testing could not discover these performance bugs in advance. Hardwired connections to other legacy applications within the customer's enterprise compounded the problem. Minor changes in the ASP application could cause malfunctions in the connections to other applications. As the number of connections

multiplied, the risk of unexpected malfunctions increased exponentially. Experiencing these difficulties, ASPs became almost as gun-shy
about enhancements as their more traditional application brethren.

Such a posture leaves customers vulnerable in an environment
characterized by accelerating technology innovation and growing
business uncertainty. A key component of flexibility is the ability to
adapt to new technology capabilities and new business needs. This
often requires rapid changes in the functionality of applications.
Any company that fails to make these changes will be vulnerable to
new entrants who can leapfrog existing technology platforms to
exploit new opportunities.

By implementing Web services architectures, ASPs will meet
this customer need much more economically. They will do this in
two ways. Leveraging the component elements of the architecture
and the loosely coupled interfaces with other applications, ASPs
will much more easily develop new functionality in one part of an
application without worrying about malfunctions created in other
areas. ASPs will also enhance functionality of existing applications
by identifying creative new applications developed by others and
plugging them into their existing applications. In this way, they
can leverage product development investments made by others
and focus more tightly on the functionality of their core application. In both cases, customers will benefit from the ability to access
the most up-to-date functionality in the quickest and most cost-
effective manner.

All these lessons point to a much more fundamental lesson. Many
companies that drove the first wave of ASP deployment viewed the
Internet as a powerful new distribution channel for existing applications. The real lesson from the difficulties experienced by this pioneering wave of companies is that the Internet is not simply a new
distribution channel. It often requires a fundamentally new set of
products and technologies if a business is to exploit its full potential.

Very few of the first wave of ASP developers adopted Web services architectures. However, those ASP developers that used related,
Internet-based application technology (e.g., applications designed
for "thin" clients with object-oriented programming techniques)

tended to fare better than those ASPs migrating traditional enterprise architecture technology to the Internet. Few have yet achieved profitability, but the economic trajectory is more comforting. Significant lessons emerge by comparing the performance of this small subset of ASPs with the broader experience of the first wave of ASPs.

Web services architectures are the key to unlocking the full business potential of the Internet. Without actively embracing these architectures, the vision of application software delivered as a service will remain a flawed vision. The vision itself is compelling. The real need is for a technology platform that makes the vision a reality. Once this is in place, the vision can be extended and harnessed to deliver real business value.

PART II

Finding Near-Term Profitability

4

Pragmatic Adoption
of Web Services

BUSINESS MANAGERS are justified in cringing when they hear
about a new technology. Vendors make expansive claims about
new technologies, and yet the business benefits are often elusive.
Even worse, new technologies often mean significant investments
at the outset (usually even more than anticipated) and long lead
times before any meaningful business impact appears. The adoption process often seems like a roulette wheel—put your money
down, hold your breath, and hope that, when the wheel stops spinning, you actually end up with more than you put down.

Web services offer a different proposition. Unlike many other
technologies in the past, Web services represent a highly pragmatic
technology, one that requires limited investment at the outset and
quickly yields business impact. This attractive business proposition
makes it likely that Web services will be broadly adopted by enterprises. As discussed, Web services address compelling business
needs regarding flexibility and collaboration better than any existing technology architectures. By addressing these needs with limited investment and short lead times, Web services can overcome
the natural resistance of business managers to yet another technology platform.

There are reasons to be optimistic about the pace of the adoption of Web services. Nevertheless, the pace will ultimately be
determined by several factors, in particular the service grid that

provides the foundation of a robust Web services architecture. These factors will be especially important in determining how rapidly businesses adopt Web services to support mission-critical business processes. The service grid must include specialized enabling services to provide the performance required by these business processes. Businesses will need to agree on a standard language to establish automated connections across business processes. Moreover, business managers will need to evolve technology and business platforms within the enterprise to harness the full potential of a Web services architecture.

In the longer term, the adoption of Web services will accelerate because of strong network effects. Network effects exist when the value of a product or technology increases as the number of people using it grows. For most software products, network effects are relatively minor. For example, the value of an enterprise resource planning (ERP) application like materials requirement planning to the enterprise is not much different if one or one thousand other enterprises are using the same application. Web services are different. The value of Web services rises exponentially as more and more enterprises adopt this technology.

The Pragmatic Adoption Path

Business managers who have lived through the implementation of enterprise applications speak graphically about the challenges. A major investment typically must be made at the outset. For a large enterprise, the investment can run into the billions of dollars. Even for midsize enterprises, hundreds of millions of dollars can often be involved. Of course, the software itself is only a small part of the investment. Businesses must put forth substantial effort to adapt the software to the enterprise and, conversely, adapt the operations of the enterprise to the software. As a result, significant lead times are usually required before meaningful business impact can be realized. Five- to ten-year implementation programs are common. And then, when it is all over, business managers can start to reap the rewards—maybe. Business managers will be relieved to hear that Web services offer a very different adoption profile.

Dell's early experience with the implementation of Web services illustrates the pragmatic adoption path offered by this technology architecture. Dell became interested in Web services as a way to coordinate more effectively with business partners in its supply chain. As Dell grew, it accumulated a broad range of assembly plants, each operating on its own distinctive set of legacy applications. These plants relied on third-party logistics companies, called vendor-managed hubs, to collect and maintain inventory from all its component suppliers. The vendor-managed hubs shipped to the plants in accordance with weekly demand schedules from Dell.

Dell had a strong economic motivation to improve the efficiency of this supply chain. Direct materials, the components used to assemble Dell's products, represented as much as 70 percent of Dell's revenue. Even modest savings in direct materials could translate into significant bottom-line impact. Equally important, Dell faced significant economic exposure in its component inventories. In an industry in which product prices have been declining at an average of 0.6 percent per week, components purchased this week tend to be more expensive than components purchased next week. If Dell or its suppliers hold inventory for long periods, then they must bear not only the cost of capital tied up in the business, but also the price disadvantage of products made or purchased earlier, when prices were higher.

The challenge, of course, was that greater efficiency in the supply chain required more coordination with many other enterprises, starting with the vendor-managed hubs and moving out to a much broader community of suppliers spread around the globe. These enterprises all had their own hardware and software platforms, representing many incompatible systems. The level of technical sophistication also varied widely across these enterprises.

Dell operated with a five-day "ship to" target, from the time it received an order by a customer to the time it shipped the order. In contrast, Dell's suppliers operated with fulfillment lead times of forty-five days. Before implementing a Web-services-based solution, Dell relied on three mechanisms to meet its ship-to targets. First, it maintained a twenty-six- to thirty-hour inventory buffer at its assembly plants to help ensure smooth assembly operations.

Second, it required suppliers to maintain ten-day inventory buffers at the vendor-managed hubs. Finally, it distributed a fifty-two-week demand forecast on a weekly basis to suppliers. The system worked, but only with large inventory buffers and the resulting economic penalties. These penalties were tolerated as insurance to guard against unexpected shifts in demand and the resulting supply/demand imbalances.

Dell resolved to reduce these penalties as much as possible by improving coordination with its supply-chain partners. It started by seeking to reduce the twenty-six- to thirty-hour inventory buffers it maintained at each assembly plant. Using supply-chain application software purchased from i2 Technologies, Dell began issuing new manufacturing schedules for each of its assembly plants every two hours. These manufacturing schedules reflect all the changes in customer orders occurring in the previous two hours. They specify what specific components are required to supply the operations of the assembly plant and instruct the vendor-managed hubs to arrange to deliver these components to specific buildings and dock doors, so that the components can be immediately moved to the appropriate assembly line.

The manufacturing schedules are published as Web services via Dell's extranet. The component specifications are sent in an XML format so that they can directly interact with the various inventory management systems maintained by the vendor-managed hubs. The vendor-managed hubs have implemented the capability to respond to the component orders automatically through the extranet. They then have ninety minutes to pick, pack, and ship the required parts to the assembly plant.

The results of this automated Web-services-based approach have been impressive. Dell has reduced the component inventories at its assembly plants from twenty-six to thirty hours of production to three to five hours, a reduction of more than 80 percent. In an interview in 2001, Eric Michlowitz, director of supply chain e-business solutions for Dell, highlights an additional benefit: "What we've been able to do is remove the stockrooms from the assembly plant, because we are only pulling in materials that we need specifically tied to customer orders. This enabled us to add in additional production lines, increasing our factory utilization by one-third."

But Dell did not stop here. One temptation for large customers is to push back inventory holding to its suppliers. This doesn't reduce inventory holding in the supply chain; it merely shifts it from the customer to the supplier. Dell realized that to increase the efficiency of the supply chain and make the system more cost-effective, the company would have to help its supply-chain partners reduce their inventory as well. This led to a second wave of initiatives focused on reducing buffer inventories in the vendor-managed hubs.

Buffer inventories at the hubs had been necessary because of errors in the demand forecasts and uncertainties about component availability from suppliers. Dell addressed these issues by checking on the reliability of supplier delivery schedules early enough in the process to allow effective contingency planning and avoid unanticipated disruptions in supply. For example, if notified early enough about a shortfall in the supply of components for a specific computer model, Dell could temporarily withdraw that model from its Web site. This illustrates the types of loosely coupled compensation mechanisms that a Web services architecture can provide to support mission-critical business processes.

Michlowitz's team is deploying a Web-services-based event-management system to receive early notification of potential shortfalls in component supplies through its extranet. The approach specifies an automatic exchange of inquiries and confirmations with suppliers, which is triggered by particular events. For example, when a supplier has committed to ship an order at a specific time, Dell's computer systems automatically generate an inquiry to the supplier at that time to determine whether the order shipped as planned. Using Web services, the inquiry can interact directly with the supplier's shipping application and generate a confirmation back from the supplier, indicating that the shipment went out as scheduled.

This automated exchange of inquiries and confirmations is important for three reasons. First, it avoids the need to directly access the databases and applications of the supply-chain partner, an approach that would naturally generate considerable concern about data confidentiality and application security. Instead, the automated exchange gets the information required to adapt the supply-chain process through inquiries and relies on the supplier to respond with the specific information needed. As a result, this approach requires much less investment and lead time to be implemented. Of course, such an approach requires a substantial degree of trust between supply-chain partners.

Second, the automated exchange of inquiries and confirmations helps Dell compile a record of the accuracy of the responses by its partners in terms of their ability to perform as represented. Although Dell trusts its suppliers, it can now also verify their performance. The ease of these performance evaluations will help Dell and its supply-chain partners identify and address performance gaps collaboratively. If performance gaps persist, Dell has the option of shifting business to higher-performing suppliers. Dell could perhaps manually capture and accumulate the data required to drive this learning and evolution of the supply-chain business processes, but the cost and potential for error would be much greater.

Finally, by automating the inquiry and confirmation process, Dell eliminates significant labor cost previously required for monitoring supply-chain events. Dell can redirect employees from routine monitoring activities to focus on exception handling, where they can deal with unanticipated events that cannot be handled through predefined business rules. The automated process also compresses throughput times and increases accuracy.

When this event-management system is fully implemented using a Web services architecture, Dell projects 10 to 40 percent reductions in inventory holdings at the vendor-managed hubs. Gross margin performance will also significantly improve as the system makes possible a more effective matching of demand and supply.

Operating-cost reduction, gross margin improvement, and asset leverage through more effective coordination of supply-chain processes across enterprises are all important benefits of the implementation of Web services technology. But Michlowitz points to another benefit. "New product introductions represent one of the most potentially disruptive events in a supply chain. In a fast-moving industry like ours, Dell must manage two thousand product transitions each year. Supply-chain event management becomes essential to handle this pace of innovation."

In such an environment, product inventories run a high risk of obsolescence, with the consequent penalty of inventory write-offs, both for Dell and for its suppliers. Supply-chain event management reduces inventory exposure during new product introductions by sharply diminishing the inventory of components that must be held at each level of the supply chain. As a result, Dell and its partners can economically support more accelerated rates of innovation, which gives them a significant edge in generating revenue growth and even more margin improvement.

Michlowitz understands the benefits of the loosely coupled approach that is central to a Web services architecture. In a rapidly changing business environment, Dell needs to rapidly evolve both its own operations and its relationships with major business partners. Dell believes it must work toward ninety-day implementation cycles, and Michlowitz asserts that loosely coupled approaches are the only way to meet this kind of timetable.

Michlowitz sees another benefit: "The loosely coupled approach also minimizes the technology burden on business partners and increases not only the capability, but also the incentive, for collaboration." This approach increases the incentive to collaborate with Dell because the cost of entering into a relationship is much lower than would be the case with traditional electronic data interchange networks or proprietary connectors that can only be used to connect to Dell. Instead, business partners at most need make only modest investments in implementing Web services interfaces to their applications. The investment can be justified not only in terms of collaborating with Dell, but also with any other business partner adopting Web services technologies as a basis of collaboration. This business benefit is a direct result of the architectural principle discussed in chapter 2: Maintain simplicity at the end points of a Web services connection.

The experiences of early adopters like Dell illustrate the following characteristics of the pragmatic adoption path offered by this new technology architecture:

- Leverage existing technology investments
- Implement incrementally
- Focus on tangible early wins
- Plug in elements over time

These characteristics are discussed in the next sections.

Leverage Existing Technology Investments

Businesses do not have to rip out existing computer hardware and software to take advantage of Web services. The services can be implemented as an overlay on existing technology platforms. This means that a company need not abandon the investment it has already made in its information technology. Instead, Web services further enhance the value of this investment by providing additional capability not otherwise available. What's more, Web-services-enabled business initiatives can typically be implemented faster than can other technology platforms that often require major restructuring or other adaptations of existing systems. Finally, Web services are especially helpful in gaining the cooperation of business partners, who are understandably reluctant to adopt expensive technology platforms simply for the privilege of collaborating with a particular company.

Dell's experience illustrates the importance of leveraging existing technology investments in the context of supply-chain business process initiatives. Dell has been successful in part because it did not have to impose major new technology platforms either on itself or on its business partners. Whenever multiple enterprises are involved, each with its own accumulation of distinctive (and often proprietary) technology platforms, Web services make it much easier and faster to achieve business impact by allowing these enterprises to leverage the technology platforms already in place.

Implement Incrementally

Web services have a further advantage. They can be implemented in small increments, providing an overlay only on those specific software applications required to accomplish a particular business objective. In this way, even the modest investment required to implement Web services technology could be staged and synchronized with individual business initiatives. The investment can be explicitly tied to tangible business benefits.

This business-driven incrementalism is in sharp contrast to recent trends in the implementation of enterprise architectures that represented all-or-nothing propositions. You either redesigned all the core applications, or you were significantly penalized in terms of business benefits.

Dell proceeded in waves of implementation tied to very specific business objectives, like operating-cost reduction and inventory savings. Only the applications and databases required to achieve these business objectives were exposed as Web services. This gradualism again was important in reducing the cost of entry for Dell's business partners—the migration to a Web services architecture could be staged incrementally to reduce the up-front investment required for participation. The partners didn't have to commit across the board to a new technology architecture at the outset; they could edge their way in, gaining experience and motivation as they began to see real business benefits materialize.

Focus on Tangible Early Wins

Incremental implementation means that business managers can choose where to begin the migration to a Web services architecture. As with any other business change initiative, companies would be well advised to prioritize and sequence their actions based on a simple grid contrasting the size and timing of business impact with the size and timing of investment required to achieve the impact. By prioritizing their actions in this way, executives can help accelerate business impact while reducing early investment needs. As rapid and tangible business benefits accrue from relatively modest investment, organizations become willing to mount more ambitious initiatives that offer even larger business benefits, but require more investment and perhaps longer lead times.

Dell again illustrates this characteristic in action. Dell targeted some very substantial savings in a major area of the firm's economics. The implementation plan started with relatively simple initiatives such as compressing the cycle of manufacturing schedule releases and coordinating with a limited number of vendor-managed hubs. Once business impact could be demonstrated from these early initiatives, Dell moved on to implement more challenging programs such as the event-management system covering its major first-tier suppliers.

Plug in Elements over Time

The Web services architecture is rapidly evolving. Not all the elements (especially in the service grid) are yet available. The available elements will continue to be enhanced as many technology firms continue to innovate with new product offers. Some business managers might see the evolving state of the Web services architecture as a very good reason to stand on the sidelines and wait for the architecture to become more fully defined before proceeding with implementation. Although it is easy to understand this response, it is mistaken.

One of the virtues of a Web services architecture is that it is itself loosely coupled. New components and services can be added over time without requiring a wholesale redesign of the components and services already implemented. Similarly, existing components and services can be easily replaced by enhanced components and services. This makes it easier to be an early mover without incurring the risk of being leapfrogged by later adopters.

As Dell again illustrates, an enterprise can realize significant business value by moving now with the elements of the Web services architecture currently available. Undoubtedly, even more business value will be realized over time as new elements in the architecture become available. In the meantime, though, Dell has learned a lot about both the potential and the limitations of a Web services architecture, as well as the practices required to most effectively implement this new set of technologies. Dell can now move more quickly to implement this architecture in other parts of the business, achieving additional business benefits.

Just as with its early pioneering of the build-to-order manufacturing model, Dell is well ahead of many of its competitors in learning how to succeed in the implementation of Web services technology. Others will undoubtedly try to copy, but they will discover that they cannot simply reproduce the institutional skills Dell is now developing in this area. Companies encounter inherent lead times when they try to develop these institutional skills. Others that wish to develop the institutional skills required to harness this powerful new technology would be well advised to start now.

Of course, there is a flip side to this ability to move early in the absence of the full development of all the elements of the technology architecture. Precisely because not all elements of the technology architecture are in place today, business managers must be realistic about what is achievable with the current state of the technology. They must map out a migration path based on an objective assessment of current capabilities of the architecture. They need to avoid initiatives that depend on elements not yet available. In some cases, they may still be able to mount such initiatives by plugging in earlier generations of technology to fill the gaps. In doing so, managers need to be wary of locking themselves into proprietary extensions of the architecture that undermine its modular nature. This form of lock-in may make it more difficult to migrate to the full Web services architecture as it becomes available.

Adoption Accelerators

Web services architectures are likely to be broadly adopted, given the compelling business benefits and the pragmatic adoption path. Nevertheless, a variety of factors can help accelerate their adoption:

- Delivery of mission-critical functionality
- Development of shared meaning
- Generation of revenue from Web services
- Discovery of, and access to, Web services

By watching the development of these factors, business managers can shape their own migration path—certain applications of the technology may become feasible sooner if these factors are developing rapidly. Conversely, if the factors are taking longer to be developed, business managers will need to reevaluate the timing of specific business initiatives requiring these capabilities.

In many cases, this is not simply a question of passively watching for developments. Enterprises can play a significant role in helping to promote and shape many of these factors. This is certainly the case in developing the enterprise platforms required to participate in a Web services architecture. Companies need to acquire the tools and platforms required to expose their applications as Web services and then to manage the deployment and operation of these Web services over time. Even with regard to the service grid, enterprises have an opportunity to shape, if not participate in, the development of the specialized utilities required to build out the service grid.

Chapter 2 highlighted the importance of the service grid. In the early stages of Web services deployment, the service grid ensures the performance required to support mission-critical business processes. The grid helps define and evolve the shared meaning that a business needs to collaborate with other business partners. As Web services architectures are more broadly deployed, the role of the service grid will become more critical in helping to connect potential users and providers of Web services and in providing the tools required to generate revenue from Web services. Each of these capabilities will play a key role in driving the adoption of Web services.

Delivering Mission-Critical Performance

The specialized utilities of the service grid provide various components of mission-critical functionality: reliability, availability, and security. Without these, it becomes more challenging to use Web services architectures to support mission-critical business processes. More challenging, but not impossible.

As the Dell example illustrates, enterprises can start implementing Web services architectures even in the absence of specialized utilities. For example, Dell offered its extranet technology platform to support interaction with its business partners. By using technology built on public Internet standards and protocols, Dell was able to provide enough of the necessary reliability, availability, and security without requiring its business partners to invest in proprietary technology. Of course, if specialized utilities had been available to provide much of this functionality, Dell could have provided even more functionality in flexible ways to its business partners. Specialized utilities in areas like message transport, nonrepudiation, and security will develop deep expertise in their business area and innovate rapidly to provide enhanced functionality.

Some traditional enterprises may even have an opportunity to develop some of these utilities themselves and offer them as a specialized service to other enterprises. Large companies have sometimes established considerable expertise in certain areas of technology required to deliver mission-critical functionality. Certainly they would have much more credibility in offering such specialized services than would start-ups with no name recognition, no track record, and the long-term viability concerns typical of any start-up.

Even where traditional enterprises are not in a position to offer the specialized services themselves, they have considerable influence in drawing investment to build these specialized services. The managers of traditional enterprises can be very articulate in creating awareness of the need for such services. They also can help such services develop by offering to become beta sites and eventually reference sites for the specialized service utilities.

Developing Shared Meaning

Specialized utilities in the service grid can also play an important role in helping companies develop and refine shared meaning. As discussed, this shared meaning becomes essential to support collaborative business processes spanning a number of enterprises.

Dell played a key role in defining the XML-based standards to describe its products and their components. As discussed previously, these standards helped Dell automate much of its communication with its business partners. In the process, Dell also significantly increased its ability to coordinate activities across its own assembly plants.

Dell was able to do this because it was focused on a limited number of business partners within a particular business process. Since it had been doing business with these partners for a long time, a substantial degree of mutual understanding and trust already existed. This made it much easier for Dell to create the standards required for implementing a Web services architecture and to gain their adoption.

Dell could in effect evolve a specialized utility that would continue to refine these XML standards based on experiences with the existing implementation. In the rapidly moving computer industry with new products and components introduced on a regular basis, Dell will need to update the XML standards to reflect the changing product universe. More broadly, by observing where exceptions occur in the supply-chain process and determining whether confusion about the meaning of terms contributed to these exceptions,

Dell can play an important role in continuing to evolve the XML standards for the benefit of its business partners.

Again, the evolution of XML standards is an option for Dell, but it also may represent a distraction. Dell is in the computer business, not the standards definition business. Third parties may have an opportunity to emerge and provide specialized standards monitoring and enhancement services, supported by technology tools to automate much of this process. These third parties might also help in a related area: the monitoring and refinement of policies required for the smooth functioning of such loosely coupled systems. Like the meaning of specific terms, policies need to be simply defined at the outset and then refined as the participants gain experience with these systems. Dell can play an important role in contributing to the success of such specialized services by making available to selected third parties its deep expertise in the computer product business and mobilizing its business partners to support the enhanced standards.

Developing shared meaning is inherently a time-consuming process. It is also a highly political process in which each party may seek to shade meaning to its own advantage or simply to reflect its own unique experience. All parties must negotiate and agree on standardized terms; they must then integrate them into their systems and organizations and refine them over time as they learn where misunderstandings still occur. Companies can play a significant role in accelerating this process. Nevertheless, they must remain realistic about the time and effort required to make progress in this area. An objective assessment of progress in creating shared meaning will provide a key indicator of the pace of adoption.

Generating Revenue from Web Services

In the early stages of Web services architecture deployment, the bulk of the application services offered in this architecture are likely to be delivered as part of a broader business relationship. Dell provides an example of this early approach. Over the previous two decades Dell had already built a broader business relationship with its partners. Dell developed and offered application services because they enhanced the performance of the broader supply-chain-business process, not because they represented a source of additional revenue for Dell. Dell achieved significant inventory reductions and operating cost savings and, indirectly, enhanced innovation capabilities—these were the economic benefits that motivated Dell. As a result, Dell did not have to worry about implementing the capability to charge for application services.

Specialized companies may offer application services as their core business. As previously indicated, the next generation of application service providers is already emerging to harness the power of a Web services architecture. These specialized companies will be very focused on the capabilities required to charge for application services. Chapter 2 discussed these capabilities, including security, metering, monitoring, billing, and payment mechanisms. These are all examples of services that will be offered by specialized utilities in the service grid. Of course, these capabilities can also be obtained in more traditional forms, either as application software that can be installed and operated by the application service provider or as an outsourced service by providers using earlier generations of technology. In the near term, many application service companies will undoubtedly rely on these approaches to create the basis for a revenue-generating business.

As the specialized utilities of the service grid emerge and evolve, however, they are likely to help provide additional incentives for the growth of application service businesses. Although traditional approaches are available to implement revenue-generating capability, they are often expensive and inflexible. Specialized utilities offering these capabilities in a Web services architecture will be able to deliver these capabilities as lower-cost services that can be rapidly enhanced over time. This will reduce the initial investment required to build application service businesses, make it easier for them to capture revenue from their service offerings, and allow them to focus more of their resources on developing the functionality of their core offerings. As specialized providers deploy more and better application services, businesses will find more incentives to adopt the Web services architecture to get access to these application services.

This category of service grid utility may also be shaped by initiatives taken by large enterprises. As in the aforementioned examples, large enterprises may be uniquely positioned to create the specialized utilities-delivering elements that can help others to generate revenue from their application services. Chapter 2 mentioned that Citibank has exposed its payment-processing engine as a Web service. Even before the advent of Web services architectures, Cincinnati Bell developed such strong capabilities in billing technology and call-center operations that it spun out an independent company (Convergys) to offer these services to other enterprises. Large enterprises may also create additional demand for these specialized services as they discover the potential to generate additional revenue from value-added services. They will then need the same revenue-generating capabilities that specialized application service businesses require.

Finding and Accessing Web Services

In the early stages of Web services deployment, finding and accessing Web services will not be challenging. As indicated earlier, the complexity of the task increases exponentially as the number of potential services multiplies.

Certainly companies like Dell are not yet focused on this challenge. The Web services supporting Dell's supply-chain business process are few and well known to Dell and its business partners.

This lack of complexity can change rapidly, however. Without specialized services in the service grid like directories and brokers to help find and access Web services, there is a substantial risk that the adoption of Web services could stall as enterprises become overwhelmed with the growing complexity of this task. Enterprises will need to begin at an early stage to develop and integrate services to help users locate the appropriate resources in the Web services arena.

The tools to do this will certainly be offered as specialized services by utilities in the service grid. For these tools to have value, though, they must be embraced and used by the developers of Web services. As developers of many early Web services, large enterprises are especially important in helping to increase usage of the specialized services for finding and accessing Web services. In many cases, especially in the early stages of deployment, large enterprises will want to use these specialized services only within their own private trading networks to help their business partners and themselves make best use of the Web services being deployed. Over time, however, it may make sense to offer many of these resources to a broader range of businesses, particularly as enterprises begin to exploit the potential for generating revenue from Web services.

Network Effects

Challenges also represent opportunities. As mentioned, the proliferation of Web services as adoption expands challenges enterprises to find and access the best and most appropriate resources for a specific business need. The specialized services emerging to help enterprises deal with this challenge will, in the process, transform this challenge into an enormous opportunity.

As more and more Web services can be found and accessed, other companies have more incentive to adopt this architecture. Powerful network effects take hold as each wave of new adopters develops and offers its own Web services, making adoption even more compelling for the next generation of adopters. Of course, all software businesses enjoy a limited form of network effect through their ability to amortize a large up-front investment in the development of the software product across an expanding customer base. This form of network effect is limited because the value comes from amortizing fixed costs. Some of this value may get passed on to customers in the form of lower prices, but the software provider typically captures a substantial portion of the value.

Web services enjoy an additional form of network effect. As more Web services become available, customers receive increasing value because of the growing range of functionality that can be accessed and combined in tailored ways to address specific business needs. Specialized enabling services that help enterprises find and access appropriate Web services can mitigate the potential costs of complexity created by increasing variety. In this case, the value is first and foremost to the customer, although Web services providers also benefit by more rapid adoption of the basic platforms required to create and consume Web services.

The incentives created by network effects help draw in new participants to the Web services architecture. They also work to expand the participation of enterprises that have already adopted Web services technology in part of their business activities. The increasing number and variety of Web services available to address a much broader range of business needs will encourage early adopters to expand their use of a Web services architecture.

Network effects will also help accelerate the development of shared meaning. As more and more participants adopt standardized forms of shared meaning, each new enterprise will have stronger incentives to quickly adopt the same standards. Part of the incentive stems simply from the force of numbers—once a critical mass of participants employs specific standards for communicating, the use of those standards becomes even more compelling for the next wave of participants. The incentives will also be increased largely by the experience and learning achieved by the early participants. Any standards for communication in a Web services architecture are likely to be rough at the outset. Experience, and learning from that experience, will help enrich the standards and increase the conviction that these standards can effectively handle the most challenging business conditions.

Of course, network effects create double-edged swords. Once a critical mass of participants adopts the platform, accelerated adoption is virtually guaranteed. But getting to a critical mass is particularly challenging. The very elements that make the platform particularly valuable when a large number of enterprises have adopted it can also make it much less valuable if only a few have adopted it. As we will see in chapter 5, the likely patterns of adoption among enterprises will work to overcome this near-term challenge and help build the critical mass for network effects to take hold. As with any network effects platform, the challenge in the early stages is to find uses for the platform that do not require a broad range of other participants already onboard.

5

Moving from the Edge
to the Core

WEB SERVICES offer a pragmatic adoption path for enterprises. Given this pragmatic adoption path, where are enterprises adopting Web services technology first? Why are they choosing these areas? Where will they apply this technology next? This chapter will focus on the likely patterns of adoption. By shedding light on patterns of adoption, the chapter will help managers determine where they might first deploy this technology and define a broader implementation program to exploit the potential of this technology. Managers will generate much more business value by moving beyond one-time implementations and pursuing a more systematic program to target the key economic leverage points of the enterprise.

As chapter 2 indicated, Web services architectures are distinctively able to enhance the flexible coordination of business processes that span various enterprises. In doing this, Web services can deliver significant operating-cost savings and greater asset leverage. The earlier Dell example is only one illustration of a broader theme: The early adoption of Web services technology will be driven by very pragmatic efforts to achieve near-term operating savings. What portions of business processes are being targeted first? As a broad generalization, many of the earliest implementations are focused on the portions of business processes occurring at the edge of the enterprise.

What is the edge of the enterprise? This can vary by type of business. It is any category of business activity involving frequent interaction with numerous other enterprises or consumers. Procurement is a classic example of an edge activity—purchasing managers must frequently interact with a broad range of suppliers. Other edge activities include sales, marketing, and customer support. As collaboration between enterprises increases, even activities like product development, which used to be relatively insulated from frequent contact with other enterprises, are beginning to enter into much broader relationships with business partners.

While Web services may first be implemented at the edge of the enterprise, powerful incentives will extend the application of Web services to a steadily expanding range of activities within the enterprise. Over time, a set of technologies that emerged on the Internet and began to target business activities at the edge of the enterprise will be perceived as a powerful new technology architecture to coordinate not only activities across enterprises, but also activities within the enterprise. Table 5-1 summarizes the business practices involved in moving Web services from the edges of enterprises to their core.

Beginning at the Edge

As enterprises begin to investigate the application of Web services technology, they are quickly drawn to focus on activities at the edge. This is not surprising, given the unique capabilities of this technology. At the edge of the enterprise, Web services technology has the most compelling advantage relative to traditional technologies.

At the edge of the enterprise, managers are most likely to encounter a bewildering variety of incompatible technology platforms operating across their business partners. Since these technology platforms are dispersed across many enterprises, there is no single management decision maker who can impose standards on the participants. Even if one company is powerful enough to impose a technology platform on all its business partners, it is often reluctant to do so because of resistance from existing partners and greater barriers for new companies wishing to form relationships with the company.

TABLE 5 - 1

Moving from the Edge to the Core with Web Services

Beginning at the Edge	Moving into the Core

• Coordinating with business partners
  - Sales channel management
  - Supply-chain management
  - Collaborative product development
 	
• Creating new edges with business process outsourcing
 	
• Sourcing edge applications from independent software vendors
  - Procurement applications
  - Electronic marketplace applications
  - Supply-chain management applications
	• Expanding across core business processes
	
	• Managing administrative processes
	
	• Integrating merged or acquired enterprises
	
	• Procurement applications
	
	• Sourcing applications from independent software vendors

Traditional technology approaches to creating connections across enterprises like electronic data interchange (EDI) are expensive and lack flexibility. These point-to-point connections also contribute to enormous complexity, especially among the smaller companies that have to adopt these connections in order to trade with larger companies. Since these smaller companies generally trade with more than one large company, they often have to adopt and manage multiple proprietary EDI platforms. These smaller companies frequently find that data transmitted through these EDI networks has to be manually reentered as it passes from their internal systems to the EDI network. The result is additional expense, time lags, and opportunities for error. As more electronic business relationships are formed, the complexity at the edge of the enterprise increases exponentially.

The edge of the enterprise is the Achilles' heel of traditional enterprise architectures. These architectures developed with the assumption that most of the coordination activity would occur within the enterprise and that few links would be required with other enterprises. Because Web services technology emerged in large part to help enterprises cope with the escalating complexity at the edge, it is not surprising that the early adoption focused on these edges. The next sections discuss the various ways companies are adopting Web services at the edge of the enterprise.

Coordinating with Business Partners

Chapter 4 described the initiatives by Dell to increase the efficiency of its supply chain through the deployment of Web services technology. Dell's efforts focused on strengthening the coordination with suppliers and third-party logistics companies delivering components to its assembly plants. For many, it is not surprising that Dell has emerged as an early adopter. From its earliest days, the company has developed a reputation as an innovator, driving technology to reshape key business processes to serve customers better.

Dell's broader innovations in business processes have inspired many other, much more traditional companies. General Motors has studied Dell and embarked on a multiyear effort to redesign its own supply chain. GM's build-to-order business initiative is very ambitious; it attempts nothing less than a fundamental reconfiguration of the processes for manufacturing cars that shifts from the build-to-stock approach that Henry Ford pioneered in 1914.

GM is staging this business initiative. The first stage is focused on increasing the performance of its existing build-to-stock business processes. It will then move to strengthen its order-to-delivery processes, working to further shorten the lead times from the time the customer orders the car to the time it is delivered. Finally, the company will implement build-to-order processes designed to enable customers to more easily order customized vehicles and receive them quickly and reliably.

The ultimate payoff is enormous. GM's long-term goal is to cut in half its $25 billion inventory and working capital investment. By staging this approach, GM can shift its information technology (IT) architecture and business processes incrementally, focusing only on the changes required to deliver economic payback at each stage of deployment.

Web services technology is playing a key role in driving the first stage of GM's ambitious program. To strengthen its order-to-delivery processes, GM must coordinate much more effectively with its dealer network to increase visibility for dealers throughout the network. Often, a dealer can significantly shorten the lead time required to deliver a car to a customer by simply checking the inventory of cars at other GM dealers to determine who might have the available stock. Sometimes the dealer will call around to a few other dealers to check, but the process is time-consuming and a hit-or-miss operation. It would be far better for the dealers to have an automated inventory checking process that could operate across a broad range of dealers and GM facilities.

But here's the rub. GM has a network of more than eight thousand dealers in North America alone. These dealers have installed a broad range of technology platforms to run their operations. Many dealers still have very limited IT skills in their own operations. In this environment, the ability of dealers to connect more effectively with key GM systems without substantial investment of their own is critical. Mark Hogan, the president of eGM, a business unit created by General Motors to oversee its consumer initiatives, is clear about the need. In an interview in 2001, he stated: "If we can't offer a substantial and rapid business payback to our dealers, they won't adopt the platform."

Equally important is GM's ability to increase functionality rapidly in frequent increments. Hogan has become an early and strong advocate of Web services architectures. He insists that "conventional IT architectures simply aren't up to the task—Web services architectures provide the only way to rapidly enhance IT platforms." Since the applications will be delivered as Web services, they can be easily and economically upgraded at the central Web server rather than the company's having to send out upgrade software to thousands of dealers and worrying that some dealers might still be operating on older versions of the software.

GM has seen the benefit of Web services in providing flexible connections across enterprises. The company has been able to quickly gain the support of its dealers, implement the necessary systems rapidly, and demonstrate quick payback. Since implementing this Web-services-based system, GM has reduced delivery lead times by 40 percent and improved delivery-date reliability from 65 percent to more than 80 percent.

GM has adopted Web services in other areas of its operations. In addition to developing closer relationships with its dealers, the company is also focused on developing closer relationships with its customers. GM's innovative OnStar service offering is one of the most significant initiatives in this area. Currently available to over one million subscribers, OnStar enables the driver to access a versatile voice and data wireless network to obtain a variety of services, from roadside assistance to help in locating particular addresses.

Hogan describes how a Web services architecture enabled the rapid evolution of OnStar: "GM couldn't have predicted accurately the range of services OnStar might eventually encompass—a Web services architecture allows us to rapidly innovate and build upon our early lead in this area." For example, if GM discovers that subscribers value shopping information services more than financial information services, a Web services architecture makes it easier to recruit and integrate additional shopping information service providers. Since interfaces are based on XML and Simple Object Access Protocol (SOAP) standards, GM and the new service providers will not have to develop proprietary point-to-point connectors, but instead can integrate new services into the OnStar offering much more quickly and at lower cost. The speed and low cost of integration make it easier to recruit new service providers and to experiment with new services. If proprietary point-to-point connectors were required, both GM and new service providers would think long and hard before deciding to add a new service to OnStar.

Dan McNicholl, the CIO for GM North America, also recognizes the power of moving incrementally with Web services architectures. He outlines a phased migration approach, but he understands that key elements of Web services architectures, including such basic building blocks as XML standards and segmented approaches to security, are still evolving. He is managing the migration through incremental stages geared to the evolution of the architecture itself. In an interview in 2001, McNicholl was clear on the end result: "It is not a question of whether we move to this new architecture, but when."

Dell started using Web services in its supply-chain operations connecting with suppliers and third-party logistics providers. GM, in contrast, has started at the other end of the business. It is using Web services to coordinate more effectively with dealers and purchasers of its cars. Over time, it plans to use Covisint, the consortium it established with Ford and DaimlerChrysler, to extend this technology architecture to its relationships with suppliers. The starting point may differ, but the pattern is clear: Start at the edge of the enterprise. This is where the technology challenges are often the greatest and where Web services can achieve significant business impact by coordinating more effectively with business partners.

Creating New Edges

Corporations are beginning to rethink what activities need to remain within the enterprise. Under growing competitive pressure to deliver best-in-class performance in all areas of business activity, corporations are increasingly willing to contemplate shedding activities for which they cannot achieve best-in-class performance. Companies have even shown a willingness to shed entire business processes for which they cannot establish competitive advantage.

An entire new industry has emerged under the rubric of *business process outsourcing* in response to this business trend. Perhaps the most prominent example of business process outsourcing involves the growth of electronics manufacturing services (EMSs), which provide outsourced manufacturing services to computer and telecom companies. Manufacturing processes are not the only ones affected.

Business process outsourcing firms tackle a broad range of business processes, including logistics, customer support, subscription management, billing, and transaction processing operations (e.g., credit-card processing). In addition, business process outsourcing firms support a variety of administrative processes, such as human resource management and real estate management. Some of these processes are already clearly at the edge of the enterprise, but others, like manufacturing, transaction processing, and human resource management, are typically regarded as "back-office" operations with limited contact with other enterprises.

Whenever a company decides to outsource a business process, the process becomes part of the edge of the enterprise. Management now faces the same coordination challenge presented by any other edge activity. Although the company doing the outsourcing typically has only one outsourcing provider, the degree of coordination is typically much higher than for most other business partners. Since the business process being outsourced must be closely coordinated with other activities within the enterprise, the frequency of interaction between an outsourcing company and its outsourcing provider is usually quite high.

It is precisely for this reason that many companies are reluctant to outsource key business activities. They realize that it can be much more challenging to coordinate activities across enterprises than within a single enterprise. If the coordination fails, it can be a bet-the-company proposition. The coordination challenge has many dimensions, some of them organizational and some technological. In the technological dimension, the primary challenge has been one of integrating IT systems. With traditional IT architectures, if the outsourcing company and the outsourcing provider were not using the same IT platforms, information exchange became very difficult. If the outsourcing provider has only one customer, this can be managed—the outsourcing provider adopts the same IT platforms as its customer. Of course, the provider almost never has only one customer. Outsourcing providers must serve a large, and growing, number of customers. They simply cannot afford to replicate the IT platforms of each customer. Until the advent of Web services, the response to this dilemma typically involved some combination of manual data exchange (e.g., fax and phone calls) and hardwired, electronic, point-to-point connections. For the company concerned about coordination difficulties, these common responses were typically not very reassuring.

Web services architectures provide much more flexible and low-cost connections to support outsourcing relationships. Rather than forcing either partner to switch to the technology platforms of the other partner, Web services architectures focus on connecting the existing platforms quickly and at low cost. Both partners are free to modify and change their technology platforms within their enterprises because Web services architectures are flexible enough to adapt to whatever new platform is introduced. Web services architectures also help address the concerns of potential outsourcing companies regarding lock-in and the potential viability of outsourcing providers. Since proprietary connections are not involved, the outsourcing company can switch from one outsourcing provider to another at lower cost.

EMSs like Celestica, one of the fastest-growing companies in the business, are using Web services architectures to address a difficult coordination activity in outsourced manufacturing. It is difficult enough to outsource manufacturing when a stable product line is involved. The challenges mount when large numbers of new products are introduced. Of course, there must be a seamless handoff between the product development engineers in the outsourcing company and the manufacturing engineers in the outsourcing provider. But the real payoff comes from having both groups of engineers collaborate at an earlier stage of product design, so that the design of the product can be shaped in ways that can have a significant effect on the cost of manufacturing the product. Sometimes simple (and to the customer, invisible) design changes in the product can have a major impact on manufacturing costs. It is in everyone's interest to have these design enhancements made as early as possible in the product development process.

This opportunity is certainly compelling in the high-tech industry. Product introduction cycles are short, and are continually compressing. Competitive pressures require very aggressive pricing. Celestica annually introduces more than fifteen hundred new products designed by its outsourcing clients into its manufacturing operations. As a result, Celestica is implementing a collaborative product development platform offered by Alventive, which will enable its own engineers to collaborate more effectively with its clients' engineers. This product development platform is implemented with a Web services architecture to facilitate connections across enterprises. The collaborative approach has cut design cycle times by more than one-half, by addressing such time sinks as a 50 percent error rate in bills of material generated by product development engineers. By identifying cost-saving design enhancements earlier in the design cycle, the collaborative approach also promises to substantially reduce the costs associated with manufacturing products.

We have just discussed two business processes: product development and manufacturing. One could not imagine two processes more likely to be considered internal processes with limited interaction with other enterprises. Yet, as the Celestica example illustrates, the decision to outsource manufacturing operations suddenly brings both processes to the edge of the enterprise. Both processes now experience all the challenges that more traditional edge activities have confronted. The shift of a typically internal business process to an edge process is likely another area for early implementation of Web services architectures, given their unique capabilities to connect diverse technology platforms more flexibly.

Sourcing Edge Applications from Independent Software Vendors

The Celestica example illustrates another promising area for the early implementation of Web services architectures. Powerful economic incentives are likely to drive independent software vendors focused on providing edge applications to adopt Web services architectures. Edge applications must connect many enterprises in order to deliver any value to users. Examples include procurement, the electronic marketplace, and supply-chain management.

Providers of these applications have many reasons to adopt Web services architectures. Their value depends on connecting many enterprises to a single application. Web services architectures provide a compelling way to connect these enterprises much more quickly and at lower cost than conventional technology architectures accomplish these tasks.

Many of these applications began by helping users make more efficient transactions, but the providers have found that there is much more value for users if the applications can help coordinate the business processes that surround these transactions. This creates a need to substantially and quickly expand the functionality of these applications. The providers can choose to develop the additional functionality themselves, or they can bundle this functionality from other providers who already have related applications developed. In an environment characterized by more cautious venture capitalists and public markets, these application providers must leverage their funding as much as possible. They are also discovering that customer acquisition costs are higher than expected and that significant effort is required to encourage customers to increase their usage of the application even after it has become available. Given this additional demand on resources, many of these application providers are likely to outsource as much of the functionality of an application as possible in an effort to focus scarce internal resources on customer acquisition and development. Again, a Web services architecture would help connect applications sourced from third-party developers in much quicker and more cost-effective ways.

Commerce One and Citibank provide one early indicator of this trend toward outsourcing by application providers. Commerce One was an early provider of electronic marketplace software, which helps businesses to more effectively purchase indirect goods. The company discovered not only that customers wanted to use the platform to execute a purchase, but that they also wanted the ability to conveniently pay for purchases. Commerce One could have decided to develop a payment-processing application of its own. Instead, it turned to Citibank, a company that already had deep expertise in electronic payment-processing systems. Citibank developed Citi-Connect, an extension of its core electronic payment-processing platform, using Web services technology to automate connections across multiple existing application platforms. Machine-readable XML messages provide the "glue" connecting the functionality of market exchange platforms like Commerce One's Global Trading Web with the CitiConnect application and Citibank's Global Settlement Network, consisting of a variety of specialized automated clearinghouse (ACH) networks.

An enterprise using a market exchange platform like Commerce One's Global Trading Web can preregister information about authorization levels for specific employees and corporate bank accounts to be used for payment on purchases. When a purchase is actually made, the purchaser clicks the CitiConnect icon in Commerce One's platform. At this point, the application automatically assembles an XML-based message containing payment instructions, including the amount involved, the identity of the purchaser, the identity of the supplier, the bank that funds are to be withdrawn from, and the bank that the funds are to be transferred to, along with details regarding the timing of the payment. The XML message is then automatically routed according to predefined rules to the appropriate specialized settlement networks. This approach significantly increases the convenience for the purchaser by knitting together a variety of preexisting applications using Web services standards and protocols.

The benefits for both buyers and sellers are compelling—sellers reduce the time required for settlement by 20 to 40 percent, and both buyers and sellers reduce their settlement costs by 50 to 60 percent. Citibank benefits by building existing operational capability into a new service line, which reaches a broader range of customers through platforms like Commerce One. Commerce One also benefits. By providing the users of its Global Trading Web access to value-added services from highly credible providers like Citibank, Commerce One eliminates the need to develop these services itself. Instead, the company can focus on signing up more buyers and sellers, using value-added services like Citibank's as an additional draw for buyers and sellers to move more of their transaction activity online. Commerce One understands the value of this relationship. It is aggressively recruiting other companies to offer value-added services like integrated logistics services on its market exchange platform.

Moving into the Core

Once Web services architectures are implemented at the edge of the enterprise, it is only a matter of time before they spread into other parts of the enterprise. Four main avenues of expansion are likely to play a role in the spread of Web services architectures.

Expanding across Core Business Processes

For reasons already discussed, Web services architectures are particularly well suited to address the needs of business processes located at the edge of the enterprise, where coordination across multiple enterprises is particularly challenging for traditional technology architectures. As companies deploy Web services architectures in their business processes at the edge, the architecture will have a natural tendency to expand into broader segments of the same business process.

Let's take an example. Procurement is a business process at the edge of an enterprise. It is also part of a much broader core process within the enterprise—manufacturing and logistics—that involves all the activities associated with the movement and transformation of physical products from supplier to customer. Once a Web services architecture has been implemented for procurement, business managers will begin to see value in broadening the deployment of the architecture to coordinate activities across the full scope of the broader core process. Often, the activities encompassed by this broader core process are supported by legacy applications that are difficult to integrate. In this case, a Web services architecture can provide an overlay of technology to create much more flexible and low-cost connections than would be possible with traditional enterprise architectures.

Even where a company has unified all the applications within the core process through a conventional enterprise architecture, a Web services architecture can help create additional flexibility. Processes and applications evolve. Web services can provide a feedback loop based on monitoring how exceptions are handled and, as a result, can determine how the process rules can be refined. Web services can also help companies access new or improved applications without incurring the expense to hard-wire them into the existing enterprise architecture.

Dell found that its initiatives to use Web services platforms in coordinating supply-chain business processes quickly expanded to its assembly plants. To coordinate with its supply-chain partners, Dell also had to improve coordination among its assembly plants. Given their rapid growth and geographic expansion, Dell's assembly plants had implemented their own manufacturing applications and database management systems without regard for the need to coordinate with other plants.

Rather than imposing a major redesign of the systems' architecture, which would have required all its plants to adopt the same technology platforms, Dell chose a different approach. The company used the XML framework in the Web services architecture to define a common name for each part, module, and subassembly used in its plants, along with a common way of describing the key attributes of each product component. Once Dell created this common language within the XML framework, machine-readable electronic documents associated with the supply chain (e.g., a bill of lading) could be exchanged between any of Dell's assembly plants and Dell's supply-chain partners. In addition, Dell could more effectively coordinate its assembly plant operations to manage any local supply/demand imbalances. Thus, Dell's adoption of Web services technology, originally focused on improving coordination with supply-chain partners, quickly expanded to include the databases within its own assembly plants.

Managing Administrative Processes

Web services architectures will not only expand within core business processes; they will also begin to expand into the administrative processes of the enterprise. These support processes—human resource management, financial management, facilities management, and IT management—tend to be shared across core business processes. As these support processes begin to interact with Web services architectures within the core business processes, opportunities will emerge to extend this architecture into the administrative processes. Precisely because these support processes need to interact with a broad range of applications and data supporting the core processes, managers of these processes will see value in establishing the more flexible connections enabled by Web services.

As an example, let's look at sales—clearly an edge business activity that ties into the broader core process of customer relationship management. When a salesperson makes a sale, this event needs to be communicated to the financial applications of the enterprise, and if the salesperson is on commission, the event must also be communicated to human resource management applications. These connections may already be implemented in a hardwired form if the company has adopted an enterprise architecture. More typically, the connections are fragmentary and require a lot of swivel-chair integration, whereby data is printed out from one system and manually reentered into another system. Web services architectures can help provide more-flexible and lower-cost connections than can existing technology approaches. As business managers in the administrative processes see the distinctive value of Web services architectures, they will begin to extend their use of these architectures into other parts of the administrative processes.

Integrating Merged or Acquired Enterprises

Mergers and acquisitions have a spotty record in terms of delivering improvements in shareholder value. Economic studies consistently conclude that roughly two-thirds of all mergers and acquisitions actually destroy, rather than create, shareholder value. Why is this the case?

Generally, senior managers seek two kinds of economic benefits when they make the decision to merge with, or acquire, another company. Most frequently, they assume that they will achieve significant operating-expense savings and greater asset leverage by integrating the business activities of the two companies. Occasionally, they also believe that they can accelerate revenue growth, either by increasing bargaining leverage with distribution channels or by offering customers a more attractive bundle of products and services from the two merged companies.

Whether it is cost savings or revenue growth, these economic benefits can only be realized through rapid and effective integration of business operations. Of course, many organizational factors work to undermine the integration of business operations. However, as any manager who has been through a major merger or acquisition can testify, the need to integrate the IT systems used by both companies represents one of the biggest challenges confronting postmerger integration. Since two companies rarely use the same technology platforms, the technology integration process can be very challenging.

Using conventional technology approaches, this integration often takes far longer and costs a lot more than anticipated. In many cases, the challenges presented by the integration of major legacy applications can deter management from actually exploiting some of the cost savings or revenue opportunities initially projected. In other cases, management may simply decide to force standardization on one company's technology platforms, creating significant business disruptions as major parts of the merged enterprise seek to migrate to a very different technology platform. Given the enormous challenges in postmerger integration of IT systems, the decision to acquire another company may be influenced by whether the two companies have compatible IT systems.

Web services architectures can significantly alter this picture. By deploying the loose-coupling capabilities of Web services architectures, managers can much more quickly and economically link the technology platforms of the merged enterprises. At a minimum, the use of Web services architectures will reduce the cost of this linkage and will accelerate the enterprise's ability to reap the anticipated economic benefits from a merger or an acquisition. More likely, Web services architectures will increase the economic benefits generated from a merger or an acquisition by reducing a major obstacle to postmerger integration. In the process, Web services architectures will become more pervasive within the merged enterprise, connecting a broad range of technology platforms in all areas of business activity. By increasing the probability, timing, and amount of economic benefit achievable, Web services architectures may also play a significant role in increasing the economic incentive to undertake even more mergers and acquisitions.

Sourcing Applications from Independent Software Vendors

Earlier in this chapter, we considered the strong incentives for providers of edge applications to adopt Web services architectures. These architectures are likely to be adopted by a broader range of independent software vendors (ISVs) over time. Enterprises increasingly source their major business applications across the enterprise from ISVs, rather than developing them internally. Thus, the choices made by ISVs regarding their approach to application development will indirectly shape the application architectures of their customers.

Established ISVs in general have mixed incentives with regard to the adoption of Web services architectures. The vendors will likely be attracted by the opportunity to establish faster and more cost-effective connections to other applications. On the other hand, they may perceive some potential threats to their business from Web services architectures.

At the most basic level, ISVs have developed considerable expertise in traditional technology architectures and will be reluctant to develop skills in a new set of technologies. In particular, ISVs that have been successful in building a leadership position will likely be complacent about the need to master a new technology platform.

These vendors also will be concerned about the potential for increased switching by their customers. If connections with other applications are easier to establish, customers unhappy with one

ISV are likely to find lower switching barriers in moving to a provider that can better meet their needs. Indeed, this ease of switching may be a powerful motivator driving customer adoption of these architectures.

Customer switching out of core applications is not the only concern. Leading ISVs in the enterprise application category have grown substantially in the 1990s by offering broader suites of related applications. These application suites have had considerable appeal to customers, who realize that it has been difficult and expensive to knit together applications sourced from different vendors using previous generations of technologies. Web services technology changes all that. As it becomes easier to mix and match applications from multiple vendors, customers may find broad application suites less and less appealing, particularly since these suites cannot be best-in-class in every application category. The result may be elimination of a key growth vehicle for ISVs in the future.

Established and successful ISVs are also likely to have mixed feelings about the pricing implications of Web services architectures. Although customers can certainly continue to purchase software licenses and install applications on their own premises, a growing number may be attracted to the opportunity to source these applications as a service, which would spread their payments out over time and tie them more closely to actual usage of the application. ISVs that have become used to large up-front payments for their software are likely to resist a shift to service-based pricing, given its potential for substantial near-term erosion in revenue generation.

For all the reasons that an established ISV could be reluctant to move aggressively to Web services architectures, new ISVs may perceive a significant competitive opportunity. By adopting Web services architectures as their core technology platforms, these new ISVs may be able to exploit the vulnerabilities of established players. New ISVs can use Web services architectures to reduce implementation costs significantly, since their applications would be much more easily customized and connected to existing legacy applications. Thus, new customers would find the offerings of the new ISVs much more compelling than those of established ISVs in terms of implementation costs. Since the new ISVs would have a minimal installed base of customers, they would presumably be less concerned about lowering switching barriers for existing customers.

A similar calculus applies to the opportunity to adopt service-based pricing models. New ISVs typically look for ways to reduce barriers to adoption. Large up-front licensing fees often represent a significant barrier, particularly when a software provider does not have a large installed base of reference customers. By offering a pay-as-you-go monthly usage fee, new ISVs can encourage trial and create the potential for significant annuity revenue streams longer-term. Since they don't have a large installed customer base, new ISVs would be much less concerned about the sharp drops in near-term revenue that can occur as a company shifts from up-front payments to monthly charges.

New ISVs would also find Web services architectures attractive in terms of their ability to rapidly enhance functionality. This would allow new ISVs to get into market much more quickly and use the capabilities of Web services architectures to rapidly and economically implement new functionality within their core applications. The ISVs could also more easily plug in incremental functionality available from more specialized software providers, thereby leveraging their own product development resources and sharpening their focus on core applications. New ISVs would find the need for rapid enhancement of functionality far more compelling. New software providers face a daunting competitive challenge when confronting established ISVs with more mature products incorporating a broader range of functionality. Web services architectures would give these new ISVs a quick and cost-effective way to close the functionality gap with established ISVs.

The dynamic thus becomes clear. The first ISVs to adopt Web services architectures will be the providers of edge applications for which the distinctive capabilities of these architectures can generate the most value. These early pioneers are likely to be quickly followed by a wave of new entrants targeting established application software categories within the enterprise. These new entrants will adopt Web services architectures because of the competitive advantage they can provide and because these companies do not have large, installed bases of customers to protect. As these new entrants begin to make inroads into the market because of their ability to better serve customer needs, established ISVs in all major application categories will find themselves forced to migrate to Web services architectures, both because their competitors offer them and because their customers are demanding them. As this process plays out, more and more of the application portfolio of the enterprise will be available on Web services architectures.

At the end of the day, a new technology architecture that first emerged from the "cloud" of the Internet will reshape the technology platforms of the enterprise. Too many executives narrowly view Web services architectures as a technology platform that sits outside the enterprise while the enterprise itself continues to operate on conventional enterprise architectures.

As we have seen, the first entry point of these architectures into the enterprise will be at the edge of the enterprise, where the business needs are greatest and where the distinctive capabilities of the architectures are strongest. This is only an entry point. The deployment of the architectures will not be contained there. The business needs are so compelling and the advantages of the architectures so clear that business managers will rapidly expand the reach of these architectures to all corners of the enterprise.

In the process, these architectures will reshape the entire technology platform used by enterprises to run their business. Existing technologies will remain largely in place, but the relationships between these technology platforms will be redefined through a Web services architecture overlay. The overlay will help managers get even more value out of their technology and business assets.

The quest for significant operating-cost savings and enhanced asset leverage will drive the initial implementation of these architectures. So far, the implementation efforts have been highly opportunistic. A manager under pressure to deliver more operating savings somehow hears about Web services technology. Often encountering significant resistance from within the organization, the manager persists, finding someone with expertise in the technology and supporting an implementation program. These one-time initiatives deliver impressive results.

But, as this chapter suggests, enterprises can implement this technology much more broadly within the enterprise during this first stage of migration to reap more substantial rewards. Working in parallel with executives pursuing one-time initiatives, senior management needs to begin crafting a broader implementation program systematically identifying the most fruitful areas for near-term operating savings. Systematic and focused efforts will likely accelerate the implementation of this promising new technology and deliver more substantial and more immediate operating savings to the business.

In the process of generating these business benefits, however, Web services architectures will lay the groundwork for a different kind of business opportunity. Aggressive managers who realize the potential of these architectures will use them first to focus the enterprise more tightly and then to execute leveraged growth strategies. Parts 3 and 4 describe the real economic prize offered by Web services architectures.

PART III

Creating Focus

6

Process Networks

Creating Value through Specialization

PART 2 DISCUSSED some of the early patterns in adopting Web services architectures. One key message came through loud and clear: Early adoption will be driven by the ability to deliver tangible operating-cost and asset savings quickly and with limited investment. But to paraphrase a popular song, Is that all there is to Web services? Are we simply talking about just one more way to drive cost out of business? Or is there more?

Part 3, beginning with this chapter, will make the case that there is far more to Web services. Although cost-reduction incentives will drive the early adoption of Web services technology, the real economic payoff from Web services will come in a very different form.

Cost reduction is essential for a business's survival in markets characterized by increasing competition, but by itself it is not sufficient. If companies focus exclusively on cost reduction, most of the savings will get "competed" away and captured by customers. As this process unfolds, the revenue of the enterprise will steadily shrink. The only way to continue to create economic value in this environment is to find major new sources of profitable growth. This section explores a prerequisite for growth—tighter focus on areas of best-in-class performance—and the key role that Web services can play in restructuring business activities to support this drive for tighter focus.

In the middle of an economic recession, few companies will have the appetite to launch aggressive growth strategies. Nevertheless, senior management will be reassured to know that, in the process of seeking further cost reduction, it is laying the foundation to support more aggressive growth in the future. Some more ambitious companies will realize the broader potential of Web services technology and begin to map out promising growth strategies now. Chapter 9 will make the case that all companies should at least have some explicit perspective on their long-term growth opportunities in order to focus their near-term cost-reduction efforts.

Whether pursuing near-term cost reduction or longer-term growth opportunities, management must also realize that new technology alone cannot create economic value. Businesses must change how they operate. This is the only way to effectively exploit the potential that new technologies offer in terms of economic value creation. Though true for cost-reduction initiatives, it is even truer for growth initiatives.

The rest of this book will explore the many levels of change that businesses must undergo in order to fully exploit the potential of Web services technology. Companies today are still at a very early stage in the implementation of Web services technology, focusing exclusively on very basic operating-cost reduction and asset savings. As a result, the examples of innovative approaches to business will largely come from companies that have not yet adopted Web services technology. In these cases, we will show how Web services technology could make the innovative approaches even more successful.

There is a key message here. Executives need not wait for the further development and deployment of Web services technology to begin to gain early experience with more flexible and focused approaches to business. At least some businesses are demonstrating that it is possible to move ahead of the technology. Of course, new technologies will only help amplify and accelerate the impact from these business initiatives. Those who have already gained some experience with the new business approaches will be in the best position to exploit the capabilities of these new technologies.

But, we are getting ahead of our story. Let's begin by reviewing some early efforts to craft a new set of business relationships that we would describe as *process networks*. So far, these business relationships have been laboriously constructed and maintained without the benefit of Web services architectures. As we will see, Web services architectures can help reduce investment and increase returns in these process networks.

Some Early Process Networks

When they see that we're going to discuss Cisco and Nike, many readers will immediately have an allergic reaction. Haven't we heard enough about these two companies? What more can be said? Aren't they both struggling now? What can we possibly learn from these two companies? These are all fair questions, but don't stop reading now.

Several aspects of both these companies have received little attention in the press. With Cisco, everyone has focused on its approach to contract manufacturing and supply-chain management, not on Cisco's approach to managing the demand chain—the complex network of highly specialized business partners that Cisco mobilizes to increase the value of its own products to its customers. In fact, Cisco has adopted a rather different approach to managing its demand-chain partners (i.e., resellers and a variety of value-added service providers) relative to its supply-chain partners, and these differences appear to be paying off.

When the press talks about Nike, it tends to focus on the company's success in building a global brand and carving out a leadership market position in the highly volatile athletic shoe business. Or, the press focuses on Nike's challenges in responding to allegations of oppressive labor practices in some of its suppliers from developing countries. What the press usually overlooks is Nike's broader efforts to design and orchestrate a global network of suppliers to help itself cope with the volatility of its shoe business.

Let's look at Cisco first. Cisco began with a key strategic advantage—it deployed a large direct sales force, calling on large corporate customers to sell its high-end router and other networking products. Besides being a major barrier to entry for other networking product vendors, this direct sales force knew its customers' needs in great detail and helped Cisco anticipate new product opportunities. This knowledge shaped both Cisco's internal product development efforts and its technology acquisition programs.

As Cisco grew, its distribution channels evolved. Sales of lower-end router and networking products to small and medium-sized enterprises represented a major new source of growth for Cisco. To reach these customers, Cisco found itself increasingly dependent on a large network of third-party resellers. Though economically necessary for reaching smaller enterprises, these resellers were worrisome from a strategic perspective. They tended to guard their customer relationships jealously, often refusing even to provide Cisco with the names of their customers, much less any information about their needs. The resellers were also able to sell other competing networking equipment, reducing the barrier to entry that Cisco had carefully constructed with its direct sales force.

In response to this challenge, Cisco devised a strategy based on an innovative Internet platform called Cisco Connection On-line. Cisco invested heavily in marketing to make both actual and potential customers aware of this online resource. The Web site itself was designed to be very helpful to corporate customers, offering them detailed product information on Cisco's broad and increasingly complex product line as well as decision tools to help customers decide which Cisco products were best suited to their needs. Of course, to use these tools, the customers had to provide Cisco with information about themselves. For example, to decide on the right network configuration for a customer, the product configurator would ask about the size of the customer, the volume and nature of its network usage, and the broader technology infrastructure within which the products would operate. In addition to enabling Cisco to help the customer with expert advice on the right equipment configuration, this information could be captured by Cisco in a central customer profile.

Using this information, Cisco could then decide which of its thousands of highly specialized channel partners would be most helpful to the customer. In addition to focused resellers, Cisco could refer the customer to specialized consultants, vendors of complementary products, systems integrators, installation services, training services, and maintenance services. In each case, the channel partner would receive a highly qualified lead and the customer would receive tailored support to maximize the value of Cisco products. And Cisco would remain the unique owner of an increasingly rich profile of each corporate customer.

Now, many companies have developed complex and highly structured distribution channels to reach the customer. What sets Cisco apart from most others is the degree to which it has emerged as an explicit and systematic orchestrator of its channel partners, tailoring the specific configuration of channel partners to the individual needs of each customer. It performs this role not just for one level of distribution, but also for many levels of support, both pre- and postpurchase. In the process, Cisco has recaptured significant strategic advantage, both in terms of its unique access to integrated customer profiles and in terms of an increasingly rich network of channel partners that can add tailored value to the customer.

Nike provides an example of a similar development, but this time focused on the supply-chain side of the business. Nike's key business challenge involved coping with a highly volatile fashion business—the athletic shoe product line. Fashions rapidly and unexpectedly emerged and just as rapidly and unexpectedly vanished. Product volumes for specific models could skyrocket and then plummet. Market demand was uncertain, but there was also considerable uncertainty regarding tariff levels and other trading regulations in countries around the world. These tended to change frequently and unpredictably, significantly affecting the cost of a shoe delivered to a retailer. At a much earlier stage in its development, Nike confronted the extreme uncertainty that a growing number of businesses are experiencing. As a result, it needed to create around the world a highly flexible network of production partners that could help it cope with this uncertainty.

Few people realize that Nike does not manufacture any of the shoes that carry its logo. Instead, the company has developed a highly differentiated network of production partners (Nike uses this term, rather than suppliers, to highlight the importance of business partnership) to meet its needs. James Brian Quinn, in *The Intelligent Enterprise*, provides insight into how this differentiated network operates.

First-tier production partners assemble the finished shoes and sell them directly to Nike. Nike segments this first tier into three broad categories, with each category optimized to a particular product need.

Its top category of production partner—developed partners—is focused on producing the leading-edge, and most expensive, models of Nike shoes. These tend to be relatively low-volume lines. Nike works closely with these partners in terms of collaborative product development (often pushing shoe technologies to their performance limits) and coinvesting technologies.

The second category of production partner—volume producers—usually focuses more on high-volume shoe lines and often develops a specialization in certain styles of shoes. These partners tend to be more vertically integrated, and they cope with the volatility in volume by working for other customers in addition to Nike.

Finally, the third category of production partner—developing sources—tends to be focused on the more margin-sensitive shoe lines, for which the ability to take advantage of low labor costs is most critical. As a result, these partners tend to be focused in less-developed economies like China, Thailand, and Indonesia. They usually produce exclusively for Nike, and in return, Nike works with them to upgrade their capabilities in a "tutelage" program so that they can evolve into higher-level categories of production partners.

That's just the first tier. Nike also works closely with second- and third-tier partners—those who provide materials, components, or subassemblies used by first-tier partners in delivering finished shoes to Nike. In effect, Nike has become very adept at orchestrating complex, multilevel networks of production service providers on a global basis. The controversy over labor practices of some of its production partners should not obscure the power of the network Nike has created. In fact, the flexibility created by this network can ultimately help Nike address many of the concerns regarding labor practices. Just as it imposes strict standards on the quality of its products, Nike can also enforce stricter standards regarding labor practices. With the flexibility created by this production network, Nike can reward production partners that observe these standards with more of its business and penalize those who violate these standards by shifting business out of their operations.

What Is Different about Process Networks?

Process networks unlock the real economic value of business collaboration. Business collaboration has become a cliché—everyone talks about it, but there exist precious few examples of its generating real business value. The problem is that the idea of business collaboration is too abstract; it can mean everything or nothing. Is it collaboration when any two companies engage in a commercial transaction? Is any business partnership a collaboration?

Business collaboration generates meaningful economic value only when it focuses on enhancing the performance of specific business processes that extend across multiple enterprises. Process networks become the mechanism that achieves this performance improvement. As the preceding examples illustrate, *process networks* are expanding groups of companies organized by an orchestrator across multiple levels of activity in a business process to improve performance. The core business processes addressed by process networks include customer relationship management, supply-chain management, and product innovation and commercialization. As discussed, Cisco created a process network focused on customer relationship management, whereas Nike's process network focuses on supply-chain management.

Process networks are very different from the business-to-business marketplaces that captured the imagination of so many business managers in the first wave of Internet commerce. Business-to-business marketplaces focus on facilitating transactions, helping to connect buyers and sellers, and providing transaction-processing support. Marketplaces typically focus on only one stage of a much broader industry value chain. Although these marketplaces can provide a valuable service, their value may have been significantly overestimated. The truth is that, with the exception of trading companies, most of the economic value of a business is concentrated in the processes that surround a transaction, rather than in the transaction itself. Process networks focus on improving the performance of business processes across many levels of an industry value chain. In this way, they can provide far more value than business-to-business marketplaces can provide.

Most companies are developing stronger relationships with suppliers, and many companies manage multiple channels to reach their customers. Are these examples of process networks? They certainly provide a promising beginning, but they don't go far enough. Process networks are different because the role of the orchestrator extends beyond two levels of activity in the business process. In the case of a supply chain, orchestrators are making choices not just regarding their direct suppliers, but regarding the suppliers to their suppliers and even farther back into the supply chain. Similarly, in customer relationship management, the orchestrator is not simply choosing a specific channel partner to reach a customer, but configuring a complex network of relationships between many companies to support a specific customer's needs across multiple levels of activity.

Process networks in effect represent a very different approach to managing business processes precisely because the networks do extend across enterprises involved in multiple layers of a core business process. Traditional approaches to managing a business process begin to fall apart when multiple companies need to be organized to support a business process.

Process networks succeed because they create loosely coupled business processes that are much more flexible and can be tailored to the needs of specific products, customers, or both. Loosely coupled business processes are modular. The modules represent either work groups within a company or, in the case of process networks, entire companies. Standardized interfaces for each module enable the modules to be dynamically swapped to tailor the business process. Loosely coupled business processes today are found largely within emerging process networks. This is not the only place where they can occur. It is entirely conceivable that loosely coupled business processes will become much more prevalent within the enterprise, as well as across enterprises. Let's explore how this approach to business process management differs from more conventional approaches used by most companies today along different dimensions: roles, rules, renewal and rewards (table 6-1). The final section of this chapter will focus on the payoff: how loosely coupled business processes generate greater economic rewards than tightly coupled business processes.

TABLE 6 - 1

Contrasting Approaches to Business Process Management

	Hardwired Business Processes	**Loosely Coupled Business Processes**
	From	*To*
Roles	Controller	Orchestrator
	Limited, all-purpose service providers	Increasingly specialized service providers
Rules	Management of microactivities	Management of macroentities
	Instructions (push)	Incentives (pull)
	Full information transparency	Selective information visibility
Renewal	Infrequent benchmarking	Continuous benchmarking
	Infrequent reengineering (every 5–10 years)	Dynamic reconfiguration
Rewards	Experience effects	Growing and continuous specialization
	Diminishing returns	Increasing returns

Roles

Traditional hardwired approaches to business process management require a process manager within an enterprise. Most of the participants within the business process are presumably also within the enterprise. To the extent that there are participants outside the enterprise, they tend to be relatively limited in number.

In loosely coupled business processes, an orchestrator is key to coordinating activity. As we will see in the rules section, an orchestrator tends to be far more removed from the individual activities required for the execution of the business process relative to traditional process managers. Nevertheless, an orchestrator performs several critical functions:

- Defines the requirements for participation in a process network
- Recruits companies to participate in a process network
- Defines the standards for communication and coordination across participants, and structures an appropriate information architecture to make the process network productive

- Dynamically composes the multiple participants in the business process to tailor it to the needs of specific products, customers, or both

- Assumes the ultimate responsibility for the output of the business process

- Structures performance feedback mechanisms to facilitate learning and to improve performance

Both Cisco and Nike, as discussed earlier, perform the role of orchestrator for their process networks. The other participants in the process network play the role of service providers that are on call to participate as needed in supporting the business process. Even when these companies produce physical products like shoes or software, they assume the role of a service provider in the context of a process network. Their role is to provide a specified service to support the execution of a broader business process.

These companies cannot join a process network on their own initiative. The orchestrator serves as a gatekeeper, certifying the capabilities of the companies before they are admitted to the process network. Both Cisco and Nike have rigorous certification procedures to determine whether a company is qualified to join the process network. Once the companies become participants, the gatekeepers must regularly recertify the companies to ensure that they continue to qualify.

In both examples, the number of service providers within a process network tends to expand over time, partly because of the opportunity for increasing specialization. The orchestrators often segment the process network according to the capabilities of the service providers, as Nike did when it specified three levels of its first-tier production partners. Cisco has established even more detailed categories of service providers to support its customers. Thus, orchestrators not only certify service providers to participate in the process network, but certify them for increasingly specialized roles within the process network.

More traditional businesses also provide intriguing early examples of orchestrators. Think of the role of a general contractor in a large construction project. The general contractor coordinates the activities of hundreds of specialized service providers across many stages of construction to deliver a finished building. The general contractor may use a very different group of service providers for one type of building compared with another type of building, but, the contractor eventually develops continuing relationships with a very broad spectrum of service providers. Executive producers in Hollywood offer another more conventional example of an orchestrator. Each movie may require a very different group of specialized service providers, and the executive producer decides which service providers qualify for each project.

Rules

Since the participants within traditional business processes largely reside within a single enterprise, it is much more feasible to manage these processes through process manuals that specify in great detail the individual activities required in a business process. Such an approach may even be extended to a limited number of business participants. This works especially if one company has significant market power to enforce detailed process specifications on the other participants. Such process manuals also work if the business participants tend to do business exclusively with each other so that they can mold their activities to conform to the business process manager.

As the number of enterprises expands, this micromanagement approach becomes less tenable. Rather than managing microactivities within the business process, the orchestrator focuses on managing macroentities like entire companies, deciding which participants to involve at specific points in the process and specifying the end products required to meet the needs of the overall business process.

In certifying service providers, orchestrators rarely seek to specify the activities that must be performed by the provider. Instead, companies like Cisco and Nike are much more focused on determining whether the service provider has the skills and institutional capabilities required to deliver specific types of end products.

Each service provider decides what activities to perform in order to deliver the specified end products. If the service provider performs well, it is rewarded with more work. If it performs poorly, the orchestrator shifts work to service providers that are performing well. Performance in a process network is much more shaped by incentives like this rather than detailed process manuals. As we will see, the orchestrator does get involved in service provider activities, but more as a coach or counselor with a longer-term focus than that of day-to-day managers.

Since orchestrators are much less involved in managing the day-to-day activities of service providers, the information architecture of a loosely coupled business process is quite different from a more conventional business process. In a conventional process, managers focused on directing microactivities across the business process require full information transparency. All information about all activities must be accessible at all times for the managers to perform their role. This is why conventional business process reengineering often requires massive changes in the architectures of corporate databases. Fragmented and imperfect information becomes a significant source of process inefficiencies.

In a more loosely coupled business process, the needs for information are much more selective across the process network. Rather than full information transparency, in which all information about all activities must be accessible to process managers at all times, a process network requires selective information visibility. Selective visibility means that only certain information is provided to selected participants at the appropriate times.

Service providers need two types of operating information from the orchestrator. First, they need selective operating information to perform the task at hand. For example, Cisco provides its channel partners with leads identifying the customer and the relevant information required for the channel partner to support the customer in a timely manner. This is usually a small subset of the full customer profile collected by Cisco, but it is enough for the channel partner to be effective.

Beyond task-related operating information, service providers also need tailored capability-building programs to keep up with the evolution of broader product platforms. Cisco, for example, also provides its channel partners with regular updates regarding the evolution of its product line. This includes customized training to ensure that each channel partner has the product knowledge required to be productive in supporting the customer, given its particular specialization.

In return, Cisco needs timely information about the delivery of the appropriate end products from each channel partner. The definition of milestone events, specifying both the timing and the nature of the end product, becomes critical to the overall performance of the process network. Rather than tracking every activity by every service provider, the orchestrator requires each service provider to notify the orchestrator upon completion of a milestone event or as soon as it becomes apparent that a milestone may be in jeopardy. If a milestone is in jeopardy, the orchestrator can then call in another service provider to bring the process back on track or modify the process to minimize any disruption that might result from failure to meet the milestone. Event notification systems of this type become a critical information backbone for the performance of process networks.

Selective information visibility is technically much less challenging to provide, especially for activities that span a large number of enterprises. The real challenge in this case is a business challenge. To select which information to give specific service providers, orchestrators must have a deep enough understanding of what information each service provider requires to perform its tasks within the process network. Cisco, for example, needs to understand each of its many types of channel partners well enough to know exactly what kind of operating information would make each partner most productive. If Cisco fails to provide the appropriate information, the productivity of the entire process network suffers.

Renewal

Conventional business processes are relatively hardwired. Because the activities are specified in detail, changes to activities in one part of the process can have unanticipated, adverse consequences in other parts of the process. Tight integration of this type helps improve near-term efficiency, but there is a price to be paid. Major breakthroughs in performance are relatively rare events.

One reason for this is that performance benchmarking is typically a very time-consuming and expensive undertaking. Gathering information regarding specific dimensions of operating performance across multiple enterprises often requires large teams of highly trained operating staff, which are usually in short supply. Much of the labor is in ensuring that the performance data is comparable. As a result, major performance benchmarking initiatives occur relatively infrequently. In the absence of clear and current performance comparisons, management often loses sight of opportunities for major performance improvement.

Even if management had timely views of performance gaps, the effort required to reengineer conventional business processes still makes this a relatively infrequent undertaking. It is not unusual for companies to go five to ten years or even longer between major business process reengineering initiatives. The very factors that make hardwired business processes so efficient in the near term make them very difficult to reengineer over the longer term. Detailed specifications need to be developed for every activity in the process. Changes to process activities often require significant redesign of underlying information technology platforms that are equally hardwired and difficult to modify. Given these challenges, it is not surprising that companies often defer reengineering initiatives until external pressures mount to the point that there is simply no other option.

The renewal opportunities for loosely coupled business processes are quite different. Let's begin with benchmarking. One of the key roles of the orchestrator in a process network is to monitor the performance of the various service providers. This monitoring is essential for the effective execution of the process tasks at hand—the event notification systems track performance against predetermined milestones.

Performance monitoring also helps the orchestrator manage its own business. Cisco needs to be confident about the performance capabilities of its channel partners both to determine which channel partner is most appropriate for a particular customer need and to set customer expectations appropriately regarding the support that will be provided. Similarly, Nike must choose the right production partners for particular models of shoes and make commitments to retailers regarding price and delivery dates well ahead of production.

Given the importance of performance monitoring in process networks, it is not surprising that orchestrators quickly develop detailed performance comparisons across service providers and regularly update these comparisons based on recent experience. This performance database in effect gives the participants in a process network access to continuous benchmarking information. At any point in time, the service providers know how well they are doing relative to comparable service providers in the process network and where the key performance gaps exist. The orchestrator helps ensure that each service provider not only has access to this information but acts on it. One reason Nike established three explicit categories for its first-tier production partners is to provide both clear feedback about performance and incentives for production partners in the lower categories to improve their performance to qualify for the top category.

With the availability of this real-time performance benchmarking information, two types of process renewal become possible. In the very short term, an orchestrator can often achieve major performance improvements simply by dynamically reconfiguring the participants in the process—swapping out poorly performing participants and bringing in higher-performing participants. This does not necessarily mean that the poorly performing participants are ejected from the process network. Performance often varies by context. One participant may be the participant of choice for one type of technology environment, but may not be the best choice for another. The orchestrator can optimize performance by tailoring the participants to the particular end products required at any point in time.

That's just the beginning. Process networks provide each service provider with both the capability and the incentives to strive for much more frequent performance breakthroughs within their own operations. The real-time performance benchmarking pinpoints where performance breakthroughs can be achieved. Since the loosely coupled business process is modular, individual service providers can work on reconfiguring their own activities without worrying about broader unforeseen impacts across the entire business process. Both of these factors—the frequent benchmarking and the modular nature of process networks—enhance the capability to strive for more frequent performance breakthroughs. The incentives come from the knowledge that, if the provider doesn't achieve these performance breakthroughs, the orchestrator will award business to other service providers in the network.

What Are the Rewards within Process Networks?

Process networks only started to emerge in the 1990s, but it is already becoming apparent how process networks can create economic value. Again, it is useful to contrast the loosely coupled business processes created by process networks with more conventional business processes within an enterprise.

Conventional business processes create economic value through experience effects. As a business gets more experience with a process, it uses that experience to find ways to deliver more value at lower cost. These experience effects can also be achieved across a limited number of enterprises working together to support a specific business process. However, managers quickly encounter diminishing returns as the number of enterprises working together increases. Given traditional approaches to managing hardwired business processes, the escalating costs of complexity involved in coordinating multiple enterprises at a detailed activity level soon overwhelm any potential experience effects.

Loosely coupled business processes certainly benefit from experience effects as well, but the real economic power comes from somewhere else. It arises from the opportunity available to each service provider to increasingly specialize in the activities for which it has world-class capabilities.

Experience effects tend to be dampened when an enterprise must perform a broad range of activities. In such cases, the enterprise may be outstanding in some activities, but also may perform much worse in other activities.

Besides enabling service providers to specialize, process networks also create increasing motivation to do so. As service providers specialize, not only do they enjoy the benefits of experience effects, but these benefits are amplified by the ability to shed activities in which they are much less distinctive. Now the learning can be focused on the areas in which the provider will have the greatest impact.

Performance rapidly improves at the level of an individual service provider, but it also improves even more at the level of the process network. As individual service providers specialize and improve performance accordingly, the orchestrator can configure tailored business processes that perform at a much higher level because they are leveraging world-class capabilities at each stage of the process.

In fact, rather than encountering diminishing returns at the overall process level as the number of participants increases, process networks encounter increasing returns: The value delivered by the process network increases as the number of participants increases. With an increasing number of participants, each service provider has a greater opportunity to specialize and improve its own performance accordingly. The orchestrator also has more flexibility in tailoring the business process to the specific needs of the individual product, customer, or both.

This opportunity for increased specialization and accelerated performance improvement is ultimately the power of the process network. The development of process networks depends on the ability of the orchestrator to understand the incentives required to motivate collaboration. In the earliest stages of development, these incentives are likely to be relatively straightforward cash incentives. For example, Cisco understands that customer acquisition is one of the key expense items for its channel partners. By designing a set of marketing programs to attract customers to Cisco Connection Online, Cisco assumes much of this expense itself and allows its channel partners to spend less in this area.

Cisco goes even further. Another big expense item for channel partners involves the effort required to qualify a prospect once the company identifies one. Particularly when highly specialized services are involved, this qualification process can be very time-consuming and resource-intensive. The ratio of prospects to customers can often be a key determinant of profitability. By spending time with customers at Cisco Connection Online to determine their specific needs, Cisco takes on much of this expense as well. As a result, when Cisco forwards a referral to a channel partner, it is usually a highly qualified referral that will most likely result in a customer for the channel partner.

As a result of these initiatives, the channel partners can refocus their available cash resources on the areas in which they can add the greatest value to customers presented by Cisco. The partners' profitability is enhanced on two levels: less expense in non-value-creating areas and more high-margin revenue by the addition of more value to the customer. Now, to make this work, orchestrators like Cisco need to fully understand the different economics that drive the performance of each category of service provider. Only in this way can Cisco structure appropriate incentives to motivate companies to join the process network and to give the necessary priority to the work generated by the orchestrator.

But these near-term cash-oriented incentives are not sufficient to explain the economic power of process networks. On a near-term horizon, the total economic rewards tend to be relatively fixed and participants are faced with a zero-sum game. If one participant benefits, another participant loses. Cisco's channel partners benefit by reducing their customer acquisition expense, but to provide this benefit, Cisco must increase its own customer acquisition expense.

Powerful incentives occur when the total economic rewards expand over time. These conditions are much more likely to create win-win situations in which all participants generate increasing benefits over time. Continuous and rapid performance improvement becomes the key to unlocking these expanding economic rewards. For process networks, accelerated improvement in the practices of the network participants becomes the primary mechanism for achieving continuous and rapid performance gains.

For this reason, orchestrators invest great time and effort in becoming deeply knowledgeable about the practices of their participants. Nike has a so-called expatriate program, with which the company sends its own employees to live and work with its key production partners for several years at a time. Nike emphasizes this program to better serve as coach and counselor to its production partners, not to direct their activities. Nike also runs a tutelage program, in which it offers its third category of production partners specific development programs they can undertake to deepen their capabilities. All of these programs reflect an understanding of long-term incentives in process networks. Learning opportunities that expand the rewards for everyone are ultimately the most powerful economic incentives to motivate and retain participants in a process network.

The increasing returns unleashed by these learning opportunities will inevitably drive process networks to expand the number of participants. The more participants, the more performance bench-marking information becomes available. With more benchmarking information available, learning and performance improve. Broader process networks will tend to perform better and create more eco-nomic value than will narrower process networks. It is precisely this dynamic that will give rise to the more sophisticated process net-works discussed in chapter 8. Over time, these more sophisticated process networks are likely to overwhelm the early forms of process networks discussed in this chapter.

Technology Enablers for Process Networks

The early process networks understandably relied on earlier genera-tions of technology—it was all that was available. In fact, they have relied disproportionately on very basic technologies like telephones and fax machines because more sophisticated information tech-nologies suffered from all the limitations described earlier in this book. Electronic data interchange networks and other more sophis-ticated electronic network options invariably proved too costly and were too inflexible to support the rapidly changing needs of process networks.

Process networks can and have operated in the absence of Web services architectures. Nevertheless, these architectures will help accelerate and reinforce the formation of process networks. The capabilities of a loosely coupled technology architecture are ideally suited for the emergence of a more loosely coupled approach to business process management. In fact, this loosely coupled ap-proach will be required if a business wants to capture the real eco-nomic benefits of this new technology architecture.

Web services architectures will enable orchestrators to shift the focus of their activity. Today, with low-technology options like tele-phone and fax, orchestrators must devote substantial human re-sources to mundane coordination activities, making sure that the process network participants have the appropriate operating infor-mation on a timely basis and collecting and synthesizing perfor-mance data.

As Web services architectures are deployed, orchestrators will be able to shift this human resource investment from basic adminis-trative activities. Low-cost, flexible connections across the process networks will automate many of the information flows. People employed by the orchestrators will be able to focus more tightly on exception handling and performance improvement initiatives. Web services architectures will help provide much more systematic information to support both these efforts.

Since connections across participants in the process network will be more automated, orchestrators will have systematic records of exceptions, including the specific circumstances that gave rise to each exception. This will be an invaluable learning tool to help orchestrators. They will be better able to identify actions they can take in advance to reduce the number of exceptions on the one hand and to limit the adverse impact of the remaining exceptions on the other hand. Orchestrators will also have much more systematic and detailed performance data for each process network participant. They can use this information to provide real-time performance benchmarking feedback to the participants and to design specific performance improvement initiatives to help accelerate learning among network participants. As we have seen, the long-term economic power of process networks resides in accelerated performance improvement.

We have already indicated that executives must employ a new approach to business process management to exploit the potential of the new generation of technology. The converse is also true: The new technology will significantly amplify the economic potential of a new management approach.

––––––––––

Process networks represent an important new dimension of focus for companies. They require senior management to move beyond the boundaries of the enterprise and to become more active in influencing activities across an entire value chain. At the same time, the networks tightly focus senior management on the activities that are central to core business processes. As we will see, senior management will also need to make critical choices regarding the focus on specific core business processes. These choices will in fact redefine the nature of the enterprise and ultimately provide a platform for rapid growth.

7

Unbundle to Rebundle

PROCESS NETWORKS represent a much more flexible approach to managing across a core business process encompassing multiple enterprises. As indicated, these process networks are emerging around three core business processes: customer relationship management, supply-chain management, and product innovation and commercialization. These core business processes are tightly bundled together in most companies today.

The Unbundling Imperative

A long-term trend toward the unbundling of the conglomerates emerged in the late 1970s. This trend significantly improved performance because it created an opportunity for management to tightly focus on one business. Everyone today understands that managing a car company is very different from managing a pharmaceutical company or an entertainment company. Almost everyone will acknowledge the powerful business benefits of focus, but a person will react with surprise at the suggestion that a favorite car company, pharmaceutical company, or entertainment company is not really very focused at all. In fact, these supposedly focused companies are still remarkably diversified in a way that few executives explicitly recognize.

Within any of these more focused companies, managers are still forced to cope with major challenges in responding to the fundamentally different needs of three very diverse businesses. Some companies have already started to unbundle further and focus even more tightly on one of these three businesses, relying on other companies to provide the elements delivered by the other two businesses.

Market forces and technology innovation will accelerate and reinforce this unbundling process. In the end, executives will be forced to ask the most basic question of all: What business are we really in?

This unbundling will not necessarily lead to an increasing fragmentation of business activity. Ironically, the unbundling may be a prerequisite for much higher concentration of business activity than has ever been possible. As such, it could generate opportunities for significant creation of economic value.

Again, we are focusing on trends that began to play out many years ago, well before Web services technology surfaced. The unbundling and rebundling trends critically hinge on the ability to coordinate business activities across multiple enterprise boundaries. For this reason, Web services technology is likely to play a pivotal role in accelerating these trends. The strong presence of these trends even in the absence of enabling technologies testifies to the power of the competitive and economic forces shaping these trends.

Three Types of Businesses

Companies today, even those that consider themselves highly focused, are really an unnatural bundle of three very different kinds of businesses. While relatively few "pure-play" examples of these three businesses exist today, some early examples can be cited. Table 7-1 shows the three types of business today and summarizes the key differences across these three types of business.

Customer Relationship Businesses. The first business is a customer relationship business. This business involves identifying a segment of customers, building relationships with them, getting to know them, and using this knowledge to work as an agent on their behalf to connect them with bundles of products and services tailored to their individual needs. It generally includes many of the activities currently performed in the customer relationship management core process, with some notable exceptions discussed in the next section.

TABLE 7 - 1

Unbundling of Traditional Businesses

	Customer Relationship	Infrastructure Management	Product Innovation and Commercialization
Skills	Direct marketing	Operations	Product innovation
Economics	Economies of scope	Economies of scale	Efficiencies of speed
Culture	Service-oriented	Cost conscious	Creative culture

In business markets, FreeMarkets represents a relatively pure example of a customer relationship business. This company might be described as an independent purchasing agent. It works with large industrial companies to understand their purchasing needs for bulk products used in manufacturing—products like molded plastic and formed steel. With this understanding, FreeMarkets then qualifies vendors that can meet the performance specifications of the industrial customer. When the customer needs to make a purchase, FreeMarkets organizes a reverse auction, in which qualified vendors bid against each other to win the order.

Because FreeMarkets itself never produces any of the products involved in the auctions, it is free from any competitive conflict that might prevent it from effectively representing the customer's interests in negotiating with vendors. FreeMarkets does not take possession of, or even touch, any products purchased by the vendors' customers. Its sole role is to make sure that customers connect with the right vendors on the best possible terms.

In consumer markets, some very traditional examples of a customer relationship business might include independent general-practice physicians and personal financial advisers. A general practitioner works to understand the health needs of individual patients and then connects the patient with a very broad array of specialized medical services ranging from testing facilities to medical specialists and hospital care services. The independent physician is paid by the patient, although if medical insurance is used, other parties become involved, creating potential conflicts of interest. Whose interests are really being served? The patient's interests? The interests of the insurance company? Or, if a corporate health plan is involved, the interests of the employer, who is trying to reduce the expense of health care benefits?

Similar issues may arise with personal financial advisers. These professionals invest a lot of time in understanding the specific financial condition and needs of their clients and then connect them with a broad range of financial service providers to meet their needs. Personal financial advisers who are paid by their clients in the form of fees charged for services rendered can escape conflicts of interest in representing their clients. Advisers who receive commissions from financial service providers are in a more tenuous position.

Customer relationship businesses also exist in more commercial arenas—real estate and automobile brokers, at least those representing the buyer, are examples. These companies use a detailed knowledge of both the customer's needs and the relevant products on the market to help connect each customer with the appropriate product on the best terms possible.

Infrastructure Management. Infrastructure management businesses represent a second type of business. These businesses focus on high-volume, routine processing activities. As a result, they cover a broad range of business activities, such as the management of a complex logistics network of trucks or other forms of transportation, the management of manufacturing or transaction-processing facilities, the management of commercial real estate properties, and the management of customer call centers. The last example—customer call centers—highlights a key distinction between infrastructure management businesses and supply-chain management business processes. Infrastructure management businesses can perform most of the activities performed within supply-chain management business processes—for example, logistics and manufacturing. They also can perform some of the activities that are usually considered part of customer relationship management—for example, customer call centers used for telemarketing and customer support. A customer relationship business will likely outsource the operation of its customer call centers to an infrastructure management business but will continue to define the policies required to strengthen customer relationships through the customer call centers.

Relatively pure infrastructure management businesses are more common than customer relationship businesses. We are all familiar with Federal Express and United Parcel Service (UPS) as examples of specialized logistics providers. Companies like Celestica, Solectron, and Flextronics have built highly specialized contract manufacturing businesses. TeleTech Holdings runs customer call centers that deal with everything from subscriber management for magazines to booking reservations for airline flights.

Product Innovation and Commercialization. Product innovation and commercialization businesses constitute a third type of business. These businesses develop a deep understanding of certain technologies or market trends and focus on organizing innovative talent to come up with creative new product or service offerings. They then engage in a series of activities designed to help accelerate and spread the adoption of the product in the market. To be clear, these businesses are not always developing physical products like washing machines or cars. They may also be developing specialized services like mortgage offerings, television shows, and maintenance services for complex equipment.

Again, there are relatively few pure examples of product innovation and commercialization businesses. Perhaps the ones we are most familiar with are fashion design houses in apparel. These companies succeed or fail depending on their ability to anticipate or, ideally, shape fashion trends and quickly bring to market creative fashion designs that match these trends. The companies rarely make the products themselves, except for the prototypes seen in fashion shows.

Another example at the other end of the spectrum involves semiconductor chip designers in the technology industry. Companies like MIPS Technologies, ARM Holdings, and Rambus come up with new semiconductor chip designs, which they then license to other companies to manufacture and market as part of broader systems.

Differences in Skills

What makes these three types of business so different from each other? Let's start with their skill sets. Customer relationship businesses require direct marketing skills to reach individual customers in very targeted ways and to tailor offers to meet their specific needs. Typically, these businesses also demand a degree of consultative skill—the ability to take vaguely defined needs and to work with the customer to sharpen those needs so that they become actionable. Long-term success requires relationship management skills and the ability to move quickly from isolated transactions to a much more sustained and trust-based relationship with a customer.

Infrastructure management businesses demand an entirely different set of skills. They require strong operational skills in the design and operation of highly standardized processes. Because efficiency is a key factor for success, the ability to relentlessly reduce operating expense and throughput times in high-volume operations while maintaining quality is highly valued. Since large numbers of people are often required to operate these businesses, human resource management skills become very important as well.

Product innovation and commercialization businesses require yet a third set of skills. A deep understanding of specific product technologies or market trends is critical to success. Creativity is richly rewarded, particularly when it can generate products or services that are commercially successful. These businesses seek segment-based or mass marketing skills rather than direct marketing skills targeted to the individual customer. The ability to communicate products in compelling ways helps accelerate penetration of the market. These businesses seek to develop their skills in maximizing product line profitability, in terms of both breadth and migration over time to new product generations.

Differences in Economics

The three business types are also driven by very different economics. Customer relationship businesses are typically driven by economies of scope. It costs a lot for these businesses to acquire a customer and invest the effort required to develop a deep understanding of the customer's needs. Profitability in these businesses depends on their ability to leverage that investment in as many ways as possible.

Scope can come in a variety of forms. One form is the familiar share-of-wallet concept, both at a category level and at a broader customer level. At a minimum, customer relationship businesses strive to serve as much of the customer's spending within a category like financial services or entertainment as possible. Ideally, these businesses would like to leverage into related product or service categories the trust-based relationship they have developed with the customer. For example, a systems integrator that begins in computer systems may seek to expand its relationship with the customer by addressing the customer's telecommunications systems needs as well.

Customer relationship businesses often benefit from a different form of scope—the breadth of relationships across as many customers as possible. Businesses with more customer relationships can exert significant negotiating leverage with vendors. They can also afford to invest more heavily in understanding vendor offers and capabilities. Finally, new collaborative filtering technology that provides these businesses with an understanding of the preferences of other customers within specific clusters of purchasing patterns can help these businesses be more proactive in recommending vendor offers to a specific customer. Broader customer bases help this technology to become more effective in fine-tuning the cluster patterns.

Customer relationship businesses often have limited physical assets. Ultimately, the economics of these businesses are customer driven. Their costs vary with the number of customers served. How much did it cost to acquire the relationship with the customer? How long will the relationship last? How much profit can be generated for services rendered each year during the relationship? The answers to these questions will shape the profitability of these businesses.

Different economics drive infrastructure management businesses. Economies of scale are a key factor in the profitability of these businesses. In part, these are simply a function of the physical facilities involved. Factories, warehouses, call centers, and technology hosting facilities all tend to benefit from scale.

Even when these facilities max out on the optimal size at the level of an individual facility, economies of scale continue to operate across a network of facilities. In some cases, these may be directly driven by network economics. For example, in a logistics network, a telephone network, or even a manufacturing network, an increase in the number of sites available in the network can often significantly reduce operating costs. Companies like Federal Express or

UPS benefit by having the volume necessary to support a dense national network of facilities. This network can increase the convenience for the customer and provide more opportunities for the shipper to move to lower-cost shipping options by aggregating volume.

More generally, experience effects can drive economies of scale beyond the size of the individual facility. Recall that infrastructure management businesses focus on high-volume, routine processing activities. Because these activities are so routine, managers can learn a lot as they gain more experience with these operations. They can study exceptions that arise in the process and discover ways to make the process even more efficient. They can study variations in performance across facilities and move quickly to disseminate best practices to drive down operating cost while increasing quality and throughput times. The more volume managers generate for their facilities, the more experience they accumulate with these processes and the more opportunity they have to refine and fine-tune the processes.

These businesses are generally physical-asset-intensive. Unlike the customer relationship businesses, these businesses do not have customer-driven economics. Of course, customers still matter for these businesses, but they count only to the extent that they help improve the utilization of physical assets. Return on investment in physical assets drives these businesses. How much did it cost to acquire the assets? How long will they remain productive? How can the utilization of each physical asset be improved to generate more operating profit each year?

Finally, we come to product innovation and commercialization businesses, for which yet another set of economics is at work. Economies of scale and scope matter far less here. In their pure form, these businesses typically have few physical assets. The businesses invest heavily in creative talent, be it clothing designers, movie actors, leading-edge electrical engineers in electronics products, or leading-edge biochemists in pharmaceutical products.

Research and development (R&D) expense is the driving expense item in these businesses. Product or service life cycle profitability thus becomes the key determinant of economic performance. How much R&D investment was required to create the product or service? How long will the product or service remain viable in the market? How much operating profit can be generated per unit of product?

In a world in which product life cycles are compressing significantly, two other factors can shape the profitability of these businesses. Speed to market is critical, both in terms of shortening the development process as much as possible and then in terms of shortening the lead times required to get the product from the development team into the market as quickly as possible. Marketing programs can also be critical in accelerating adoption once the product is in the market.

Ultimately, though, the compression of product life cycles puts a premium back on the creative talent. Can the business's creative talent continue to innovate and rapidly come up with new generations of successful products to keep the profit engine working? No matter how profitable the existing products are, there had better be a stream of even better ones not far behind.

Despite very different economics, all three of these business types can be highly profitable. The key is to understand the economics of each type and manage the business accordingly. Poor economic performance can usually be traced to management choices that suboptimize the economics because of continuing efforts to straddle more than one business type.

Differences in Cultures

It's bad enough that these three business types demand different skills and economics. They also thrive in completely different cultures.

In customer relationship businesses, for example, a professional service ethic defines the culture. These businesses typically add a lot of value in terms of helping customers determine what they want or need. Having done this, they then pull out all stops to find and deliver in a timely fashion the resources required by the customer. If the service involves a high degree of customization, so be it. If it involves doing dull and tedious things like searching through endless catalogs for a specific kind of ball bearing, that's OK. If the customer really wants it or needs it, your job is to find it and make sure that it is available when expected. Nothing else matters.

Customer champions who work around standard procedures in the organization, trying to get things done when everyone said they couldn't be done, are richly rewarded. Staff members who make enormous personal sacrifices to satisfy a customer are celebrated.

This is a relationship business. The customer relationship manager is the status role in the organization. If you want to rise to the top, get into direct contact with the customer as quickly as possible and demonstrate your ability to build lasting relationships.

Now, of course, customers matter for all businesses, but they aren't as central to the cultures of the other two business types. Infrastructure management businesses are much more internally focused, precisely because this internal focus is what determines customer satisfaction. If the process is not reliable, delivers poor quality or is too costly, customers will soon flee to other providers who can meet these demanding expectations. Precisely because these processes are so routine, customers can easily compare performance across providers.

These routine processes need to stay routine. Exceptions are a dangerous sign—too many exceptions, and the profitability of the business starts to erode. The culture relentlessly seeks standardization. Infrastructure management businesses are the home of the thick process manual—every activity carefully spelled out and even more carefully monitored. Exceptions, of course, continue to occur, but the key is to deal with them quickly and efficiently and, above all, to learn from them so that the routines can be extended to cover those situations as well.

The operations manager is the position of status in these businesses. Anyone who can wring another few cents of operating cost out is a hero. Anyone who can refine the operating process to move items through faster or more reliably can look forward to a promotion. Creativity counts, but it is very narrowly focused on fine-tuning or refining the operating processes to improve performance.

In sum, what these businesses value most is predictability. Anything that undermines predictability is viewed with suspicion.

Finally, we come to product innovation and commercialization businesses. As one might expect, it is here that we find creativity, especially sustained creativity, most richly rewarded. The creative talent rules the roost. What the creative talent wants, the creative talent gets. Research facilities on the Riviera or in Monterey, California? No problem. State-of-the-art equipment? Just sign the purchase order. A team of researchers to pursue a new product opportunity? Call Human Resources, and tell them whom you need to recruit.

Again, of course, customers do matter. But, unfortunately, they generally only start paying—if then—after the big money has been spent to develop the product. Of course, market research can help a company understand what customers will buy. Even better, leading-edge customers can often be recruited to provide input into the development process itself. In the end, it takes creative talent to process this input and make the critical choices about what to include in the product and what to leave out. In some product categories, the choice is more straightforward. In others, like entertainment products or the fashion apparel business, it is far from straightforward. In all cases, the business makes a big bet on each new product introduction. Often, it is a bet-the-business proposition that must be made not just once, but repeatedly with each new product generation.

Many product businesses have made progress in customization based on more modular designs, but even these designs have limitations. If the customer wants a feature that is not already included in a module, then it is out of luck. The customer will have to wait until the next generation. In many product or service categories, excessive customization can quickly erode profitability.

Similarly, operating processes can play an important role in these businesses, but these processes are rarely tightly standardized. Creativity trumps process standardization. If a product development team comes up with a breakthrough new product, then the processes will be modified to accommodate the needs of the new product.

The Management Trade-Off

If these three types of businesses are so different on so many different levels, then why do they remain tightly bundled together in most enterprises? At the most basic level, managers face a trade-off: Should they unbundle to capture the economic benefits of greater focus or should they stay bundled to avoid the economic penalties associated with higher coordination costs across multiple enterprises? So far, the economic penalties have generally overwhelmed the potential economic benefits of greater focus.

The economic benefits of greater focus should be clear to anyone looking at the very different skill sets, economics, and cultures that drive the three different business types. How could any single enterprise successfully optimize the performance of each of these three businesses? On the contrary, most enterprises significantly compromise the performance of all three businesses by keeping them tightly bundled together. Customers may prefer something else, but the company still tries to get them to buy its products, undermining the trust required for a customer relationship business. Factory operations may benefit from greater scale, but they remain at a suboptimal scale because the company can't sell any more products, which hampers the company's ability to compete as an infrastructure management business. Creative talent may generate more value in an organization that moves quickly, but when the operating processes of the company need to be standardized, the company reduces its ability to attract and retain the creative talent required for a product innovation and commercialization business.

The economic penalties have to do with something that Ronald Coase, a Nobel Prize–winning economist, described as "transaction costs" in "The Nature of the Firm," a seminal essay published in *Economica* in 1937. Essentially, transaction costs, or interaction costs, as some would prefer, involve all the activities associated with coordinating resources—finding the resources, getting information about them, negotiating with them, coordinating their activities, and monitoring them to ensure that they perform the specified tasks. Coase argued that companies emerged to exploit situations in which, all other things being equal, transaction costs for a given set of activities are lower within an organization rather than across organizations.

Transaction costs or interaction costs are not a trivial item. In a major research study completed in 1997, McKinsey & Company quantified the importance of interaction costs in the economy. In the United States, interaction costs account for 70 percent of total labor value-added cost. Even in developing economies like India, interaction costs still account for as much as 40 percent of labor value-added cost. Clearly, interaction costs shape a significant portion of economic activity.

Coase used the famous "all other things being equal" caveat of economists. Of course, all other things rarely are equal. Even Coase recognized that diminishing returns were likely as the number of transactions increased within an enterprise. He even pointed out that these diminishing returns were likely to be encountered sooner if the transactions were very diverse. It would be hard to imagine more diverse activities than the three business types described earlier.

Nor did Coase focus on the role of information technology (he was writing in the 1930s) in reducing transaction costs. In fact, difficulties in accessing and processing information represent a significant component of transaction costs. Technology that reduces these costs will likely help reduce the penalty associated with performing activities across enterprises. The spread of digital electronic networks is likely to play a major role in systematically and substantially reducing interaction costs.

Coase also disregarded the impact of declining interaction costs for customers. The increasing ability of customers to search effectively across vendors, negotiate with vendors, and monitor performance has played a major role in intensifying competition. As a result, the penalties of suboptimizing performance by tightly bundling very different business activities together have increased. If more focused competitors emerge in the three business types just described, they are more likely to achieve world-class performance than are tightly integrated enterprises. As a consequence, unbundling into more focused businesses may not be just an option. It may become a necessity as tightly integrated companies face more demanding customers and more aggressive, focused competitors, making it more difficult for companies with suboptimal performance to compete.

Early Movement toward Unbundling

We are beginning to see the early stages of unbundling into the three more focused business types in a growing range of industries. For example, two of the biggest growth businesses in the computer industry involve contract manufacturing and systems integration. Surprisingly, few large computer companies today actually manufacture the products they sell. Since the 1990s, most computer companies, faced with intensifying competition, have shed a significant portion of their manufacturing capacity, turning it over to focused contract manufacturers. In related moves, they have also been relying more heavily on specialized logistics providers to move products out to the customer.

In the terms used earlier in the chapter, computer companies have been unbundling a major portion of their infrastructure management business and focusing more tightly on their product innovation and commercialization business and customer relationship business. Even the customer relationship businesses have been eroding in the face of the growth of focused systems-integration companies. Systems integrators have been expanding and deepening their relationships with customers, becoming trusted advisors to CIOs and helping them make the right choices on information technology platforms, source the right products, and coordinate all the activities required to effectively implement the technology.

A natural reaction might be that these developments are understandable in the computer industry. After all, these are the providers of the technology that is reshaping interaction costs—they should be at the leading edge of the changes occurring. What about more conventional industries?

The automobile industry certainly is a classic example of a more traditional industry. Even this industry shows early signs of a profound unbundling. Responding to aggressive competition from Japanese auto manufacturers like Toyota, almost all the major car companies have initiated efforts to shed a substantial portion of their component and subassembly manufacturing operations, keeping only the final assembly operations in-house. Many factors contribute to the success of companies like Toyota, but certainly one of them involves its willingness to rely more heavily on focused infrastructure management businesses. For companies like GM and Ford, as much as 55 percent of the total component costs of a car were internally manufactured. In contrast, only 27 percent of Toyota's component costs were internally manufactured.

Chrysler was the first of the major U.S. car companies to respond to the competitive challenge. It began a process in the late 1980s to increase its reliance on component and subassembly manufacturers and by the mid-1990s had moved to a profile closely mirroring Toyota. The results were impressive: Chrysler's profit per car increased eightfold, from an average of $250 in the second half of the 1980s to an average of $2,000 in the mid-1990s. This was two to five times more profit per car than either GM or Ford were generating.

Not surprisingly, GM and Ford have begun to move in the same direction. In 1999, GM spun out its Delphi Automotive Systems Corporation as a focused component manufacturer. Ford followed suit in the next year by spinning out Visteon Corporation, a $20 billion focused manufacturer of components and subassemblies.

Like the computer companies, the major automobile companies are shedding major portions of their infrastructure management businesses. Automobile companies long ago developed franchised dealer networks as focused organizations to handle the customer relationship business. Of course, these are not yet optimized customer relationship businesses, since they are generally tightly linked to a single manufacturer. Try going into a GM dealer and asking about Ford cars.

Changes are occurring on this dimension as well. They are hampered to some degree by legal restrictions regarding who can sell a car. Even so, the spread of the Internet has led to the growth of several focused customer relationship businesses generally coming from the media industry. These businesses, like Edmunds and the Kelley Blue Books publisher, are using the Internet to provide customers with even more powerful decision tools to compare automobile models across manufacturers and to find the model that best meets their needs. A growing number of automobile purchasers use the Internet to gather information about cars before purchasing from a dealer. The Edmunds and Kelley sites generate far more traffic than do any of the automobile manufacturer sites.

Do these same trends apply to services businesses? Certain segments of financial services have moved well down this path. Take the credit card business. The processing of credit card transactions represents the most significant infrastructure management business for credit cards. This activity has been largely outsourced to very large, focused transaction-processing companies. Retail banks have taken on the role of product innovation and commercialization businesses, coming up with innovative features and offers. Increasingly, affinity credit cards have become popular, offered to customers by companies or groups like Intuit, the American Automobile Association, and AARP as they seek to broaden their relationships with their customers.

Other financial services businesses are in advanced stages of unbundling. In the mutual-funds business, one set of players often designs and manages the investment portfolio, a second group of players markets the funds, and a third group processes the transactions generated by the mutual funds. Similar patterns can be seen in mortgage lending, custodial services, and corporate securities.

These unbundling trends are also appearing in some rather unexpected places. Electrical utilities were long regarded as highly traditional businesses tightly integrated across the power generation, transmission, and retail distribution elements of the business. Since the 1990s, we have begun to see a significant restructuring of this staid industry as companies have decided to focus on either power generation, transmission, or retail distribution. Both power generation and power transmission are examples of infrastructure management businesses, although they require quite different skills. Retail distribution continues to have elements of all three business types, but at least enables companies to focus more tightly on their customer relationship or product innovation and commercialization business, or on both.

The pharmaceutical industry is undergoing similar changes. During the 1990s, ten of the largest pharmaceutical companies significantly increased their reliance on compounds licensed from other companies. The share of revenue generated by licensed compounds for these ten pharmaceutical companies increased from roughly one-quarter to one-third in the six years from 1992 to 1998. Many of these licensed compounds came from companies like Amgen and Genentech, which are more focused on product innovation and commercialization. In competing for these licenses, the large pharmaceutical companies are increasingly positioning themselves as having expertise in infrastructure management businesses like manufacturing and management of drug approval processes or in customer relationship businesses, leveraging their large physician detail forces.

On the customer relationship business side, another set of focused players has emerged to intensify competition. Companies specializing in the management of pharmaceutical benefits have grown rapidly, based on their proposition of helping large enterprises more effectively manage the cost of their pharmacy benefits programs. These companies work with large enterprises to encourage doctors to prescribe lower-cost, generic options rather than branded drugs.

Most companies are still at the earliest stages of the unbundling process. For reasons outlined in the next few paragraphs, new generations of information technology have the potential to significantly accelerate and reinforce the unbundling that has already begun, and to extend it to other industries. Thus far, the unbundling initiatives have tended to focus on carving out infrastructure management businesses from existing companies.

Focused customer relationship businesses have been created in some product categories, although most of the initiatives to date have been in business markets like computers and pharmaceutical benefits management. Less progress has been made in carving out focused customer relationship businesses for two reasons.

First, customer relationship businesses are much more difficult to carve out of existing companies. They require a significant mind-set shift on the part of management to build trust-based relationships with customers. Most executives in customer relationship businesses within large companies today adopt a vendor-centric view of the customer relationship. Their job is to convince customers to buy more of a specific vendor's products. In a focused customer relationship business, they need to adopt a customer-centric view: What products and services are most relevant for the customer, regardless of vendor, and how can the company work on the behalf of the customer to get the most value at the lowest cost?

Second, developing a deep understanding of the individual customer's needs usually requires a significant investment by a focused customer relationship business. As a consequence, customer relationships businesses so far have mainly arisen only in markets in which very large purchases by the customer justify the investment required to develop this deep understanding. For this reason, business markets or affluent consumer markets have tended to be the early seedbed for focused customer relationship businesses. This will change as electronic networks and related computing and storage technologies reduce the expenditure required to acquire and manage customer profiles.

The Rebundling Opportunity

This discussion of the unbundling imperative can create a significant misunderstanding. Many may walk away with the impression that unbundling will lead ultimately to a highly fragmented business landscape with smaller and smaller enterprises. From the perspective of an executive at a large enterprise, this is not a very energizing vision. We must compete harder and harder to get smaller and smaller.

The most likely outcome is quite different, as indicated in figure 7-1. As discussed earlier, at least two of the focused business types—customer relationship businesses and infrastructure management businesses—are driven by economics that lead to high levels of concentration and consolidation.

Strong economies of scope drive customer relationship businesses. Building a trust-based relationship with a customer requires a significant investment. A powerful economic incentive exists to expand this relationship with an individual customer as broadly as possible. These businesses are also able to add more value to the customer by aggregating and analyzing customer demand. As a result, any individual business has strong incentives to expand the number of relationships that it manages.

If we look at the systems integration business, there has been a strong pattern of consolidation over time, driven more by the first type of economy of scope (that is, expanding share of wallet across different categories of technology spending). A similar pattern can be found in the realm of pharmaceutical benefits management companies driven by the second type of economy of scope (that is, expanding the range of customers covered).

Ultimately, these economies of scope may encounter limits driven by customer trust. Consumers may trust a company to advise them on their financial service needs, but will consumers

FIGURE 7 - 1

Focused Businesses Will Consolidate

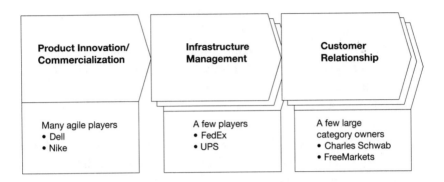

Product Innovation/ Commercialization	Infrastructure Management	Customer Relationship
Many agile players • Dell • Nike	A few players • FedEx • UPS	A few large category owners • Charles Schwab • FreeMarkets

trust the same company to advise them on their health care needs? Even within these broad limits, some very large businesses could evolve over time.

These limits may not be as hard and fast as they at first appear. They might be overcome over time through a gradual broadening of the services of the customer relationship business. A company advising consumers on financial service may include advice and help on obtaining the right health care insurance. This capability may create an opportunity to advise consumers regarding the capabilities of different health care providers. This in turn may lead to greater credibility in advising consumers regarding the pros and cons of various health care treatment options.

Economies of scale also drive infrastructure management businesses, creating similar tendencies toward concentration and consolidation. In the highly developed segments of the logistics business, for example, Federal Express and UPS have emerged as leading providers, dwarfing their private-sector competitors. Similar trends can be observed in the contract manufacturing arena, in which companies like Celestica, Flextronics, and Solectron have grown into very large and successful businesses through a combination of acquisitions and internal growth. Other segments of the infrastructure management business, like call-center operation and human resource management outsourcing, tend to be more fragmented, but they are at an early stage of development with very high growth rates.

Product innovation and commercialization businesses may be the only focused business type not subject to strong concentration and consolidation trends. Innovation and speed, usually the key drivers of economic performance for these businesses, tend to favor smaller organizational environments. Larger enterprises may have trouble delivering leading-edge performance on these attributes. It is in this business type, therefore, that we might witness increasing fragmentation, with smaller, more specialized firms prevailing against larger, slower-moving firms.

Even in this category, however, we may see some trends toward concentration and consolidation. As mentioned earlier, the fashion apparel industry is an example of relatively pure product innovation and commercialization businesses. Since the late 1990s, both LVMH and Gucci have emerged as aggregators of highly focused fashion businesses. In part, their emergence may be because both companies' specialized skills in marketing help the creative design talent get faster and broader penetration of their target markets. This kind of marketing skill may be most efficiently aggregated at the level of a corporate parent, whereas the creative design talent remains in relatively autonomous business units.

Companies driven by competency in a core technology may provide another example of opportunities for economies of scope in product innovation and commercialization businesses. A company can extend some core technology competencies to build a leadership position in a broad range of product categories. Corning has developed a deep expertise in glass technology and successfully entered and sustained positions in a variety of product categories in which glass is a key component. These categories range from picture tubes for televisions to fiber-optic cable for telecommunications networks. In 2001, Corning generated $7 billion in revenue from such products and enjoyed a market capitalization of $10 billion. Canon has leveraged a similar expertise in optical products across products ranging from cameras to copiers and printers. The company generates $23 billion in revenue and has a market capitalization of $32 billion. Of course, neither of these companies is a pure product innovation and commercialization business, but both companies illustrate the ability to innovate repeatedly across a broad range of product categories, building off a competency in a core technology.

Finding major new growth opportunities may be the only way for companies to continue to create economic value in an environment of intensifying competition. The paradox is that, in order to grow, most companies today may first have to shed significant parts of their existing business to develop even tighter focus on one of the three business types.

Tighter focus on business type does not mean more risk; it may mean the opposite. First, by tightening the focus on one business type, enterprises reduce the assets that they put at risk to create business value. Now, other companies take on the ownership of, and bear the risk of owning, some of the assets that one enterprise previously owned. Second, executives can concentrate more effectively on accelerating performance improvement in the chosen business type and reducing their vulnerability to competitors. Third, greater focus on business type can enhance an enterprise's ability to respond to unanticipated events like technology discontinuities. As discussed for process networks, executives of more focused businesses can spot potential disruptions sooner and draw on more dispersed innovation to discover appropriate responses. Finally, focusing on one business type can paradoxically be a prerequisite to diversification in terms of related products and services offered. Diversification into related products and services reduces vulnerability to market risk in the form of industry downturns or shifting consumer preferences. For example, infrastructure management businesses like outsourced customer call centers can expand to serve a broad range of industries. Even product innovation and commercialization businesses like Canon and Corning, focused on specific core technology competencies, can participate in a surprising range of markets.

The good news for business executives is that the same forces that will require this unbundling are also creating the dynamics for rebundling to build very large, and much more focused, new businesses. Even better news is that new generations of technology will make both the unbundling and rebundling much more feasible.

The Role of Technology Enablers

In the past, if one had suggested that companies would need to undergo a significant unbundling and rebundling of business activity, many executives would have been intrigued, but few would have moved aggressively along this path. Many factors held the executives back, but one of the most significant involved technology obstacles.

Many large enterprises have just migrated to massive enterprise applications in an effort to achieve tighter integration of business activities. The virtue of these applications is also their weakness. Any attempt to unbundle these business activities would have met significant resistance at the application level. The developers of these applications simply did not design them to be pulled apart and operated across enterprises, especially if the enterprises chose different application vendors.

These technology challenges have been a major inhibitor of unbundling and rebundling initiatives in the past. Given these challenges, it is surprising that any unbundling and rebundling activity has occurred at all. Over time, this picture will change substantially as technology evolves from an inhibitor to a significant enabler of unbundling and rebundling. It is here that Web services technology will play a major role, given its ability to establish flexible, low-cost connections across existing applications.

Web services technology not only helps companies shed business types and enhance coordination between the resulting independent enterprises, it can also strengthen the performance of each of these business types as they evolve into more focused entities.

Perhaps the greatest impact will be on customer relationship businesses. As mentioned, most of the unbundling to date has focused on shedding infrastructure management businesses. Creating independent customer relationship businesses can be extremely challenging on two levels. First, a business must connect with a very broad array of products and vendors to deliver value to the customer. These connections involve information access at the most basic level: How can customers quickly compare features and capabilities across relevant products or vendors? At a more ambitious level, customer relationship businesses need to coordinate across multiple vendors at an operational level to provide seamless order processing, billing, and customer support.

Second, product innovation and commercialization companies need to gain deeper insight into shifting customer preferences. For many of these companies today, the value of this insight makes them very reluctant to focus solely on product innovation and commercialization and to become dependent on other enterprises for access to the customer. Richer access to aggregated customer profiles could help a company overcome this reluctance. Product companies might gain even greater insight into customer preferences if they relied more heavily on customer relationship businesses. For example, customer relationship businesses would be in a better position to track the behavior of not just one product company's customers but also the customers of all relevant product vendors.

Web services technology can play a significant role in helping customer relationship businesses meet both levels of challenges. This technology is specifically designed to address the need for flexible and low-cost connections across a broad range of enterprises. Customer relationship businesses will be able to deliver more value more quickly to their customers as they begin to harness the capabilities of this technology.

Web services technology will be a major boon to infrastructure management businesses as well. Witness the challenges encountered by contract manufacturers in the computer industry. These manufacturers have grown by acquiring the manufacturing facilities, employees, and information technology systems of their clients. As a consequence, each facility acquired has a different set of application platforms. Simply integrating each application back into the broader application infrastructure of the customer has been enough of a challenge. Most contract manufacturers have yet to confront a bigger challenge: connecting all the applications in their inherited manufacturing facilities with each other, while preserving connectivity back to their customers. As a result, these contract manufacturers treat each facility as a completely independent operating entity. They are unable to exploit the potential economic benefits of coordinating activity across facilities, balancing available capacity against the shifts in demand from customers.

Chapter 5 provided another illustration of the potential of Web services technology in enhancing the operation of contract manufacturers. As discussed, Celestica, a leading contract manufacturer in the electronics industry, faced the challenge of handling the introduction of new products into its product line. Celestica is investing in Web services technology to create a collaborative product development platform, allowing the product development teams of their electronics clients to share design documents much more readily with Celestica's manufacturing engineers.

Market forces will make unbundling and rebundling a necessity. Technology innovations will make this restructuring much more economically feasible. As a result, the early initiatives in this direction will accelerate and expand to include a broader range of markets and industries. Executives who realize the potential use of this technology to facilitate the unbundling and rebundling of business activity and who move aggressively to restructure their enterprises to create more focused growth platforms will reap substantial economic rewards. Capturing these economic rewards will require a very different approach to growth. Again, Web services technology can play a pivotal role in driving both traditional forms of growth—organic growth and merger and acquisition activity—as well as innovative new forms of growth. In this way Web services will be central not only to the unbundling of the enterprise, but to its rebundling as well. How Web services accomplish this unbundling and rebundling is the focus of the remaining two chapters.

PART IV

Accelerating Growth

8

Creating Value through Leveraged Growth

BUSINESS IS FULL OF PARADOXES. As competition intensifies, financial markets place an increasing premium on finding new sources of profitable growth. But there's a problem. Traditional forms of growth require significant up-front investment with relatively long-term payoffs. These approaches to growth can often dampen profitability in the near term.

One option is organic growth, with which the company expands into new customer or product segments through the building of internal capability. This approach typically involves considerable investment in new physical facilities and hiring new people or skill building well in advance of any significant economic rewards.

For those who are more impatient, mergers and acquisitions (M&A) may offer a somewhat faster route to growth. But the price is higher; the acquirers usually must pay a hefty acquisition premium up front. Moreover, postmerger integration often takes longer than originally anticipated, delaying projected economic returns. Finally, the track record on economic value creation through M&A is discouraging; most economic studies indicate that more than two-thirds of M&A transactions destroy economic value, rather than creating it. In both approaches—organic growth and M&A—significant initial investment must be made in an environment of increasing economic pressure with somewhat speculative economic returns delivered at a later date.

What is management to do? It is not surprising that, under these conditions, managers often simply postpone growth programs. They choose instead to concentrate on efficiency initiatives to reduce operating costs and asset investments. As suggested earlier, though, this can be a losing approach, leading to a steadily shrinking business as customers capture the cost savings.

Leveraged Growth Strategies

Are there any other options for growth strategies? Some companies have been successful in applying a new form of growth strategy: leveraged growth. This approach begins with the realization that ownership of business assets is not always necessary to support growth. We are using the term *business assets* broadly to encompass intangible assets like operational skills or information as well as physical assets. If it can access and mobilize the relevant assets to support specific growth initiatives, then a business may capture the economic benefits of growth without the economic burdens of owning those assets. The trick is to understand what assets are required to address growth opportunities, who owns these assets, and what economic incentives are required to ensure that these assets can be accessed and mobilized when needed. As we will see, Web services technology can also help coordinate activities involving multiple asset owners.

Some Potential Misunderstandings

Leveraged growth can be misunderstood. First, it does not mean financial leverage in the sense of loading up on debt to finance the acquisition of assets. Such an approach may be appropriate whenever very stable cash flows are available to cover the interest payments. As many telecommunications companies have discovered, for example, the financial leverage to build fiber-optic networks can greatly increase the risk of business failure when the timing of the demand for this capacity is difficult to predict or depends on the actions of other companies. For the purposes of discussion in this book, *leveraged growth* means business leverage, not financial leverage. It refers to the ability to derive economic benefit from assets without owning them.

Second, leveraged growth does not simply refer to joint ventures or alliances, at least in the forms that are commonly understood. Joint ventures or alliances usually assume two forms: public-relations events or hardwired business relationships. It is not overly cynical to point out that many joint ventures or alliances have the life span of a press release. They are designed to create the impression of momentum, usually for the benefit of investors in one or both of the parties, but they never become operational.

Other joint ventures and alliances have more substance. They are designed to become operational and deliver real business value. In these cases, they tend to be structured in some detail and supported by carefully crafted legal documents and operating agreements. A business usually takes a long time to negotiate these ventures or alliances, which are relatively challenging to modify once implemented. Leveraged growth, on the other hand, creates a much looser form of relationship among asset owners; it is shaped by economic incentives rather than legal documents.

Third, at the other extreme, the business relationships established through leveraged growth strategies should not be confused with simple commercial transactions. They are not simply buyer-seller relationships in which goods are being bought and sold. Instead, they involve the coordination of business processes across multiple enterprises to deliver specific end products.

Finally, leveraged growth strategies recognize the need of firms to own assets. They are not some variant on the vision of virtual companies owning no assets of their own. In fact, to be effective in implementing leveraged growth strategies, companies must own significant assets, since these assets help generate the economic incentives required to mobilize assets owned by others. As discussed in chapter 7, some types of businesses are more physical-asset-intensive than others, but they all depend on some form of asset ownership for success. Deciding which assets a company must own to generate sustainable value is one of the key challenges in implementing leveraged growth strategies. The real focus of leveraged growth strategies is how to magnify the economic value of these assets as much as possible.

An Early Example of Leveraged Growth

One of the most successful examples of leveraged growth strategies at work comes from a company established in the early part of the last century in Hong Kong. Li & Fung began in 1906 as a family-run trading company selling to overseas merchants. In the mid-1970s, two brothers, Victor and William Fung, returned to Hong Kong from other pursuits in the United States to head up their family's business, which was trading a broad array of low-value products. Li & Fung at the time was serving as a broker, charging a fee for putting buyers and sellers together but getting increasingly squeezed between the growing power of buyers and the factories.

Li & Fung's response to this squeeze was interesting. It essentially removed itself as a direct intermediary connecting two levels of the value chain and redefined its role as a broader intermediary, connecting multiple levels of the value chain.

Today, Li & Fung is a cutting-edge supply-chain orchestrator. To produce a garment, for example, the company might purchase yarn from Korea and have it woven and dyed in Taiwan, cut in Bangladesh, and then shipped to Thailand for final assembly, where it will be matched with zippers from a Japanese company and, finally, delivered to geographically dispersed retailers in quantities and time frames specified well in advance.

Li & Fung owns none of the facilities involved in processing the apparel into finished goods or in transporting these products through the various stages of production. It does, however, have access to a global network of 7,500 supply and manufacturing companies possessing specialized capabilities both in apparel manufacturing and in a growing range of consumer hard goods manufacturing.

By leveraging this process network of specialized providers, Li & Fung has achieved impressive growth. In the low-growth apparel industry, the company managed to double its revenue to $3.2 billion over the five years from 1996 to 2000. Over the same period, Li & Fung's net income after tax nearly tripled. In fact, during this period of double-digit annual growth, the firm consistently delivered a return on equity over 30 percent—again remarkable for an industry notorious for its thin margins. Li & Fung's ability to operate with very limited fixed assets (the book value of fixed assets is only 5 percent of revenue) provides at least part of the reason for these high returns. Financial leverage is minimal; Li & Fung operates with a debt-to-equity ratio of 0.05. The productivity of Li & Fung's employees is also impressive. With only 4,200 people worldwide in 2002, the company expects to generate slightly more than $1 million in revenue per employee.

High revenue growth rates, even higher net income growth rates, and consistently high return on equity in a low-growth and low-margin industry—how does Li & Fung do it? The company has pursued a leveraged growth strategy. It reorganized the company, moving away from an earlier structure organized around geography to a new structure led by small, customer-centric divisions. Li & Fung's core customers are large apparel designers like Abercrombie & Fitch, Laura Ashley, and Levi Strauss. A dedicated Li & Fung division serves each of the largest apparel designers. Divisions organized around customer segments such as theme stores serve Li & Fung's smaller customers. Lead entrepreneurs run each customer-facing division. Their responsibility is to understand their customers' needs in depth and to mobilize the necessary resources within Li & Fung's process network to serve those customers. Each division is kept relatively small, averaging about $30 million to $50 million in revenue, to preserve an entrepreneurial spirit and culture.

This organizational structure focused the business on adding value for the customer. Rather than trying to build or acquire all the specialized processing and transport facilities required to service these customers, Li & Fung focused on developing an equally deep understanding of the specialized capabilities of existing businesses operating around the world. Based on its experience with the service providers across its network, the company has a detailed and current view of the performance of each service provider in a wide variety of contexts. For example, some apparel cutters may do well with coarser forms of wool, but lack the workforce skills or machinery required to maintain high quality and high throughputs for more delicate forms of wool like angora or cashmere. Li & Fung employees can discuss in great detail the operational performance of their service providers. This information helps them allocate work across the process network, but it also provides the basis for detailed performance feedback to service providers. Service providers know where they stand at any time along multiple performance dimensions.

When Li & Fung adds a processing facility to its network, it does not view the relationship as a short-term commercial one. It strives to become an important source of business for that facility over the long term, averaging about 30 to 70 percent of its production capacity. The company tries not to go below 30 percent of the partner's capacity because it believes it needs at least this level of activity to get priority attention from the partner and to have reasonable visibility into the real capabilities of the partner. On the other hand, the company tries not to exceed 70 percent of a partner's production capacity, because it wants to avoid having partners totally dependent on the company for their business. Li & Fung believes that partners can enhance their capabilities by working with other customers as well.

Like the orchestrators discussed in chapter 6, Li & Fung does not specify in great detail the activities of each partner in its process network. The company is focused on specifying end products and operational milestones to ensure that the end-customer's needs are met. Given a deep understanding of the operational capabilities of each of its partners, Li & Fung is able to tailor quickly the specific supply-chain process for each customer. As an example, StudioDirect, an affiliate of Li & Fung, begins production on a customer order within six hours after the order is entered via the Internet. The process network can also be quickly reconfigured to adapt to unanticipated events. For example, within seven days after the September 11, 2001, terrorist attacks, Li & Fung shifted production out of facilities based in potentially unstable countries to more secure facilities to ensure that there would be no disruption in supplies.

Also like the orchestrators discussed in chapter 6, Li & Fung relies on economic incentives rather than detailed contracts or operating agreements to gain access to a highly diverse array of assets around the world. These economic incentives begin with the company's ability to deliver substantial and steady business to its service providers over the long term through its deep relationships with major customers. The capabilities required to service a particular customer order drive the choice of specific service providers at any point in time. Over time, though, Li & Fung strives to maintain continuing relationships with all the service providers in its process network. This is certainly important in terms of creating appropriate economic incentives for service providers to make capacity available on a preferential basis. The continuing relationships are also important because they enable Li & Fung to maintain continued visibility into the evolving capabilities of each of its service partners.

Even more powerful economic incentives mobilize asset owners over the long term. Li & Fung offers its service providers not only substantial near-term revenue opportunities, but also long-term opportunities for rapid improvement in performance. Delivering against this promise starts with detailed performance benchmarking data gathered on a real-time basis by Li & Fung. As a participant in Li & Fung's process network, each service provider can afford to specialize in the areas in which it truly has distinctive capabilities. The service provider can then gain insight into major performance gaps and work with Li & Fung employees to understand how it can address these performance gaps. The result is a powerful platform for rapid performance improvement and the promise of greater rewards from more distinctive performance.

A Different Form of Process Network

Li & Fung shares many similarities with orchestrators like Nike and Cisco, described in chapter 6. All these companies have developed sophisticated skills in mobilizing the assets of other companies to add value in business processes spanning multiple levels of activity and many companies.

But there is one critical difference. Nike and Cisco are orchestrating process networks to add value to their own products—athletic shoes and complex networking gear. As such, they are pursuing one form of leveraged growth strategy. They have created closed process networks in which the service providers are exclusively focused on adding value to the orchestrator's own products.

Li & Fung has taken the role of orchestrator one step further. It does not make any products of its own. As a result, it can offer the services of its process network to any and all product vendors without worrying about conflicts of interest. Unlike the closed process networks of Nike and Cisco, Li & Fung's open process network makes services available to all.

This is a very different form of leveraged growth strategy. The growth opportunities of Nike and Cisco are bounded by their core product offerings. If these core products are broadly accepted in the market, then Nike and Cisco can add more value to the products through their process networks. If these core products lose market appeal, then the ability to add value through process networks declines accordingly. In contrast, Li & Fung has a much broader growth opportunity since it can address the needs of all product vendors in the categories it targets. The market share of any individual product vendor does not limit its growth potential.

Something else has happened. The core business of Nike and Cisco is not orchestration. It is the design and commercialization of products, supported by a robust process network. For Li & Fung, orchestration is not only the core business; it is the only business. The company has become a pure-play orchestrator.

In terms of the business types described in chapter 7, Li & Fung has become a relatively pure example of a customer relationship business. Its success depends on its ability to quickly understand the needs of its customers and, on demand, to help connect these customers with appropriate service providers. Notably, in this customer relationship capacity, Li & Fung is not playing the role of a conventional broker of goods, connecting buyers and sellers of products, as it did in its early days as a trading company. It is instead serving as a knowledge broker, leveraging a deep understanding of individual customer needs with an equally deep understanding of the capabilities of diverse service providers to custom-knit a business process.

Different Forms of Leveraged Growth

The Li & Fung example illustrates one of the more flexible forms of leveraged growth. Figure 8-1 summarizes a broad range of leveraged growth options.

Whether we are talking about open process networks, as in the case of Li & Fung, or closed process networks, as in the case of Cisco and Nike, these process networks have two specific characteristics. First, they have a *gatekeeper* in the form of an orchestrator who

FIGURE 8 - 1

Alternative Platforms for Leveraged Growth

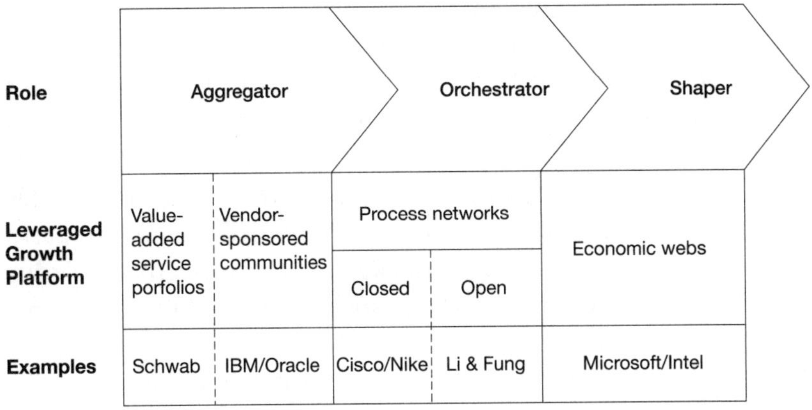

Role	Aggregator		Orchestrator		Shaper
Leveraged Growth Platform	Value-added service porfolios	Vendor-sponsored communities	Process networks		Economic webs
			Closed	Open	
Examples	Schwab	IBM/Oracle	Cisco/Nike	Li & Fung	Microsoft/Intel

determines membership in the process network. As discussed in chapter 6, the orchestrator determines who can join the process network and, over time, who can remain in the process network. All of the orchestrators described earlier define criteria required for participation in the process network and require all participants to be tested or inspected to ensure that they meet these criteria. They also periodically recertify the members to ensure that they continue to meet the criteria established. Since most process networks have different levels or categories of participation, the orchestrator will also determine the level or category of participation.

Second, these process networks bring together companies to perform specific sequences of activities within a business process. Once again, one of the roles of the orchestrator is to determine which process network participants should be involved in what sequence to execute the business process. Both the participants and the sequence of activities can vary significantly, depending on the nature of the product or the customer involved, or both. The orchestrator plays a significant role in tailoring the business process to meet the needs of specific situations.

In addition to process networks, other forms of leveraged growth are available to management as well. Two forms in particular keep the role of a gatekeeper but abandon the role of an orchestrator that specifies the sequences of activity. These forms of leveraged growth are based on resource aggregation and require an aggregator rather than an orchestrator. The aggregator determines which resources to bring together, but does not specify the sequences of resource deployment.

Charles Schwab is a concrete example of one form of resource aggregation: value-added service portfolios. It began as a discount broker offering fast, efficient, and reliable ways for investors to trade stocks. Over time, it has evolved into something quite different, using the capabilities of the Internet. On its Web site, Charles Schwab has brought together a rich array of specialized third-party resources to help its investors make their investment decisions, reproducing in many respects the capabilities of a full-service broker, but at much lower cost.

If investors want to research specific stocks, they can go to the Charles Schwab Web site and access news services like Dow Jones, company and industry reports from Standard & Poor's, and interviews with executives and industry analysts from Briefing.com. If they are interested in earnings forecasts, they can access First Call. Vickers provides insight into corporate insider trading activity, and Big Charts will provide specialized charts of stock performance over time.

If investors want more tailored information and investment advice, Charles Schwab will help connect them with one of more than five thousand independent investment managers who participate in Charles Schwab's investment network. Investors can also access a broad range of third-party investment products like mutual funds designed to meet certain types of investment objectives.

Charles Schwab carefully qualifies and monitors the performance of any third-party resource it aggregates on its site because it realizes that its reputation hinges on the quality of the resources brought together. It is up to the investor, though, to decide which, if any, of these third-party resources it wants to access. The investor also determines in what sequence it will access these resources. At this level, Charles Schwab does not play any role at all, in contrast to the orchestrator of a process network.

Let's look at another form of resource aggregation, vendor-sponsored communities. Hardware and software companies like IBM and Oracle offer perhaps the most advanced examples of this kind of resource aggregation. These companies long ago recognized that the value of their products depended on a broad range of complementary products and services. They also realized that the users of their products would derive more value if they could benefit by comparing notes with other users to learn how to better use the products in specific contexts.

For this reason, all the major hardware and software companies now sponsor both user communities and third-party communities like developer groups. User communities provide an opportunity for users to connect with each other and to learn from each other how to more effectively use the vendor's products. The vendor sponsors large user-group conferences and increasingly provides ways for users to connect with each other online. Vendors sponsor similar activities for specialized third-party communities like software developers who use the vendors' products as a platform for their own development activity. Developer groups often come together at conferences sponsored by the vendor and communicate with each other through newsletters and online forums.

Charles Schwab's value-added service portfolio helps customers connect with complementary products and services to enhance the value of Charles Schwab's own offerings. In the company's value-added service portfolio the specialized third parties do not connect with each other. They are in the portfolio to connect with customers.

Vendor-sponsored communities have a different purpose—they help groups to learn from each other. Whether it is users or software developers learning from each other, the focus is on facilitating communication within the group. The vendor gains because, through learning from each other, the various communities are able to generate more value from the vendor's products.

In these examples, the vendor plays a modest gatekeeper role, focused on maintaining the quality of the interactions and ejecting disruptive participants. The vendor plays an even more minimal role in terms of determining the sequence of the interactions among the participants. Other than structuring sessions at conferences or in online forums, the interactions are all shaped by the participants themselves.

What happens if we eliminate the gatekeeper role entirely? Are there even looser forms of leveraged growth that can be exploited by companies? Economic webs offer perhaps the most flexible form of leveraged growth. In economic webs, the role of shaper replaces the role of orchestrator found in process networks.

Microsoft and Intel today remain the most successful examples of shapers of economic webs. These companies defined and over time rapidly enhanced key technology platforms that became the de facto standards for a significant technology architecture—desktop computing. Microsoft focused on the operating system, whereas Intel focused on the microprocessor. Working together, the two companies succeeded in gaining rapid adoption of their products and, in the process, shaped an extraordinarily far-reaching and diverse web of participants who added significant value to their products.

Microsoft and Intel created an economic web based on a de facto technology standard as a shaping platform. These technology webs are the most advanced form of economic webs developed to date. Nevertheless, one can imagine other types of shaping platforms forming an economic web. For example, economic webs might form around customer profiles or standardized protocols for coordinating business relationships. Whatever form they take, shaping platforms must deliver significant functionality that evolves rapidly over time and that encourages many types of value-creation roles. The shaping platforms must generate simple but powerful adoption drivers and they must be accessible at relatively low cost (at least in the early stage of deployment).

These economic webs create much looser relationships than process networks create. Participants choose to enter or leave the web on their own initiative. The choices are largely driven by economic incentives generated by the shaping platform owned by the shaper. Shapers do not act as a gatekeeper to the economic web, directly deciding who can join. Instead, they play a much more indirect role, influencing who joins or leaves the web by the choices they make in evolving the shaping platform. These choices influence the economic incentives that in turn influence other companies' choices to participate or not to participate in a particular economic web.

Shapers play even less of a role in determining the sequences of interactions among the participants of an economic web. At this level, economic webs are much more influenced by market dynamics. For example, a customer may choose to purchase a computer directly from a systems vendor or from a specialized value-added reseller, depending on the customer's own information and preferences. Similarly, specific vendors like Compaq may create their own vendor-sponsored communities or closed process networks to mobilize specific subgroups of participants in adding value for customers. Market dynamics will determine whether these specific subgroups thrive or perish in the broader economic web.

While utilizing market mechanisms as the means of coordinating activity within the web, economic webs differ from standard commercial relationships. The shaper explicitly uses a shaping platform to harness economic incentives, mobilizing a very broad range of other asset owners to support its own business objectives. In the case of Microsoft's and Intel's economic web, the actions of hundreds of thousands of companies around the world are shaped by the choices these two companies make in evolving their shaping platform. It is precisely because so many participants are involved that economic web shapers rely more heavily on economic incentives to mobilize activity.

Benefits of Leveraged Growth

Leveraged growth offers a number of attractive benefits (table 8-1). First, it magnifies the economic value of a firm's existing assets. Using leveraged growth, management can mobilize complementary assets to add even more value to its own assets. Cisco's products are much more valuable to customers because of the vast array of specialized support services that the company can mobilize through Cisco Connection Online. Li & Fung can deliver much more customer-specific value to its apparel customers because it can access a broad network of specialized service providers.

Magnified Economic Value of Assets. Of course, these assets are not available for free. Asset owners must be paid for their services, including an appropriate profit margin. The enterprise mobilizing the complementary assets must create more value both for the customers and for the asset owners than what the asset owners could deliver independently. This ability to add value gives compa-

TABLE 8 - 1

Benefits of Leveraged Growth

- Magnified economic value of assets
- Increased returns
- Economic surplus captured through tailoring
- Reduced economic risk
    - Shorter lead times
    - Increased adaptability
    - Reduced fixed assets
    - Limited exposure of enterprise assets
- Enhanced innovation potential

nies the necessary economic incentives to gain access to the assets in the first place.

Increased Returns. Companies pursuing a leveraged growth strategy must be able to capture some of the incremental value for themselves while passing on the rest to the other asset owners. In doing so, these companies can generate higher profit margins with proportionately fewer assets than companies pursuing more traditional growth strategies. Return on assets and return on equity improve substantially with leveraged growth strategies.

Economic Surplus Captured through Tailoring. Improved profitability does not just accrue because companies can grow with proportionately fewer assets. Leveraged growth strategies can help companies hold on to more of the economic surplus because of their superior ability to tailor offerings to the specific needs of individual customers. With more flexible forms of leverage, companies can tailor pricing so that customers pay for what they really need—no more and no less. Customers often capture significant economic surplus in more standardized product and pricing markets because the vendor bundles in many features needed only by small groups of customers but then charges a lower price to reach a broader segment of the market. In such situations, many customers pay a lower price than they would be willing to pay to get access to specific features.

Reduced Economic Risk. Leveraged growth strategies can also help significantly reduce economic risk on at least four levels. First, companies can reduce market risk by accessing resources already in place in the market, without the substantial lead times often required for internal development or postmerger integration. They can move much more quickly into markets, generate revenue more quickly, learn faster, and create barriers to entry for others sooner. Second, the more flexible forms of leverage enable companies to adapt more quickly to changing market conditions. Third, companies can reduce the fixed-cost component of their operations by accessing assets owned by others. This can be very helpful in responding to unanticipated downturns in market demand. Finally, companies pursuing leveraged growth strategies reduce the absolute amount of assets they themselves must commit to pursue a particular strategy, reducing their own exposure while spreading the risk among a broader group of players who commit their own assets.

Of course, in at least one respect, leveraged growth strategies can increase economic risk. Companies pursuing these strategies must be clear about the assets they need to own to continue to generate the appropriate economic incentives required to access other assets. Otherwise, the companies risk being marginalized relative to asset owners that are much more central to the creation of economic value. Leveraged growth strategies require asset ownership. They are simply more selective in terms of the assets that a company must own to create sustainable value.

Enhanced Innovation Potential. Leveraged growth strategies also enhance innovation potential. Diverse asset owners can specialize and innovate within their area of specialization. A company can try many approaches; the ones with the greatest market value will quickly reap economic rewards as other companies seek to gain access to these sources of innovation.

Perhaps the greatest benefit of leveraged growth strategy is the most difficult to quantify in economic terms. It is the ability of management to focus more tightly on areas of distinctive competence. Ironically, the areas of the business that are performing poorly usually consume management's attention. Imagine what management could accomplish if it could dedicate all its attention and resources to deepening the existing areas of expertise and extending this expertise into related areas, all the while confident that the other elements of business value were available from equally specialized asset owners.

Integrated Growth Strategies

Most companies will want to craft growth strategies that apply many, if not all, of the variants of leveraged growth just discussed. At the same time, they should not lose sight of the role of more conventional forms of growth as well. Integrated growth strategies include the following:

- Organic growth
- Mergers and acquisitions
- Leveraged growth

Management will need to define integrated growth strategies that exploit the unique capabilities of each form of growth.

Take the example again of Li & Fung. As adept as it has become in mobilizing the assets of others, it continues to pursue more conventional forms of growth. The firm expanded its regional office network during the 1980s to reach beyond its core geographic focus of China—it first moved out into the broader Asia-Pacific region and then into more distant areas like Africa, Mediterranean Europe, and Latin America. As it demonstrated the success of its orchestration skills in the apparel industry, Li & Fung moved to expand its focus from apparel to other consumer goods requiring labor-intensive manufacturing—including hard goods like home products, furnishings, sporting goods, toys, and travel goods.

This expansion of business focus in part required organic growth. Li & Fung had to broaden its own skills in understanding customer needs from a relatively narrow and well-defined set of customers to a much broader and diverse set of customers. The company also had to broaden its skills in orchestrating supply chains for products with characteristics different from apparel's. For example, these products often required higher value-added services for smaller order sizes than were typical in most apparel products. In its organic growth, Li & Fung focused on building the specific organizational skills that were critical to its success as an orchestrator. Of course, the organic growth challenge was significantly reduced because Li & Fung could rely on specialized service providers to perform the various specialized activities required in the supply chain itself.

Li & Fung has also used acquisitions to support its growth strategy. For example, in 1995 it acquired Inchcape Buying Services, a company almost as big as Li & Fung and its biggest competitor. This acquisition helped Li & Fung to more rapidly expand its customer base in Europe and broaden its service-provider relationships to areas like India and the Caribbean. By applying its specialized orchestration skills to Inchcape's customers and service providers, Li & Fung rapidly increased the operating margins in the acquired operations.

In 1999 and 2000, Li & Fung acquired its three largest competitors. Each of these acquisitions helped Li & Fung magnify the economic value of its own distinctive asset—its organizational skill at orchestrating complex supply-chain networks—by more rapidly expanding its network of relationships with both customers and service providers.

Each of the major forms of growth played a distinctive role in Li & Fung's integrated growth strategy. Organic growth played a particularly important role in expanding the company's core organizational skills from one product category into related product categories. This helped substantially increase the addressable market for Li & Fung, thereby significantly increasing the economic value creation potential of Li & Fung's core asset.

Acquisitions helped magnify the value of these core organizational skills within the apparel product category. Through acquisitions, Li & Fung could access new customers and new service providers more rapidly than it could if relying exclusively on organic growth, although organic growth also played an important role here as well. Li & Fung quickly added value in each of these acquisitions because it applied its distinctive organizational skills to the relationships that had already been established by the acquired companies.

Meanwhile, Li & Fung relied on the orchestration of an increasingly diverse process network to access the specialized facilities and skill sets required to serve the supply-chain needs of its customers. Focusing tightly on its customer acquisition and coordination role, the company steadily deepened its capabilities through a combination of organic growth and acquisitions. In the process, it added even more value to its customers and service providers. As potential customers perceive greater economic value by working through Li & Fung, customer acquisition through organic growth will likely accelerate. Similarly, as service providers see greater benefits by affiliating with Li & Fung's process network, the growth of the process network is also likely to accelerate, creating a powerful, virtuous cycle.

The Role of Mergers and Acquisitions

As the Li & Fung example illustrates, mergers and acquisitions will continue to play a significant role in supporting leveraged growth strategies. However, these transactions will be very different from the mergers and acquisitions that have dominated the business news in the 1990s. In sectors as diverse as banking, telecommunications, energy, the media, and entertainment, we have witnessed a steady progression of mergers and acquisitions.

Unlike the M&A activity that dominated the news in the 1960s and early 1970s, these transactions do not diversify into unrelated areas of business activity. The transactions of the 1990s were much more defensive in nature, focusing on the need to quickly cut operating cost in response to intensifying competition. In some cases, as in the example of the media and entertainment, the transactions were also driven by a defensive desire to increase negotiating leverage relative to two developments: the growing power of creative talent and the consolidation of retail distribution channels. Although the M&A programs created much larger entities in the process, that was not the primary goal of companies pursuing these M&A programs. Their goal was to preserve and protect their existing business against growing pressures on profitability.

To the extent that these transactions remained largely confined to a single industry, they at least maintained the existing business focus of management, rather than diluting management attention across multiple industries. Nevertheless, building on the points made in the previous chapter, they had relatively little impact in terms of increasing management focus on one of the three major business types—customer relationship businesses, infrastructure management businesses, or product innovation and commercialization businesses. Instead, they merged existing hybrid enterprises into even larger hybrid enterprises. In the process, they made it even more difficult to unbundle into one of the more focused businesses. Management attention became focused on integrating the merged entities, rather then unbundling them. Perhaps this is why the track record for economic value creation through acquisitions has been so abysmal. Attempts to reduce operating cost through acquisitions may buy some more time than would simply reducing operating cost within a single entity, but the end result is still the same—most of the cost savings get competed away and captured by the customer.

Contrast this conventional M&A approach with a more growth-oriented M&A strategy driven from a more focused business platform. As just described, Li & Fung has pursued an active M&A strategy, but it is much more opportunity driven. The company has developed a distinctive competence in orchestrating loosely coupled business processes across multiple enterprises. It uses acquisitions to rapidly expand its relationships both with customers and with service providers. This allows Li & Fung to leverage significant economies of scope as a very focused customer relationship business. Similarly, several companies, like Solectron, Convergys, and Federal Express, more focused on the infrastructure management business, have used acquisitions to leverage significant economies of scale and to broaden their service offerings into related areas of infrastructure management. Although these acquisitions also seek to reduce cost, they primarily seek to deepen focused expertise and to expand the distinctive value offered to the customer.

The Role of Outsourcing

The discussion of leveraged growth strategies has largely been silent about outsourcing. What role does outsourcing play? As conventionally practiced, outsourcing is a much less flexible way to gain access to complementary assets relative to the various forms of leveraged growth. Outsourcing relationships are typically bilateral relationships negotiated between an outsourcing service provider and individual clients. Each relationship is generally specified in great detail, supported by hefty legal documents and extensive service-level agreements. As such, outsourcing performs much more like the joint ventures and alliances described earlier—the process requires long lead times to become established and is very difficult to modify once established.

Despite these disadvantages, outsourcing can play a significant role in helping management tighten its focus on distinctive areas of competence. In this regard, outsourcing facilitates the unbundling of the enterprise as described in chapter 7. In the process, it helps create the conditions that a company needs to pursue leveraged growth strategies that involve rebundling itself as a much more focused entity.

Outsourcing will continue to evolve into forms that are much more compatible with leveraged growth strategies. Outsourcing began around discrete business activities like warehousing and call-center operations. Over time, it has expanded to include entire business processes like logistics or customer support. The result is one of the major growth areas today—business process outsourcing. The major business process outsourcers today generally perform most of the activities within the business process themselves. Even today, though, many of these outsourcers are finding it helpful to connect with other more specialized providers for some of the activities that particular customers might need. As the ability to coordinate business activities across enterprises improves, many of these outsourcers will likely evolve into much more specialized orchestrators, coordinating specialized service providers across much more flexible process networks. Li & Fung may in fact provide a model for a new generation of much more loosely coupled business process outsourcers.

The Role of Technology Enablers

By now, readers may be anticipating the role that more loosely coupled technology architectures can play in supporting the move to leveraged growth strategies. These strategies seek to access and mobilize, in much more flexible ways, the assets owned by other enterprises to create even more value for customers. Clearly, information technology can play a major role in enhancing the capabilities to pursue these strategies. Nevertheless, new generations of technology are neither necessary nor sufficient to at least begin down the road of leveraged growth.

These strategies have often been successfully implemented within the constraints of previous generations of technology. Li & Fung, for example, relies on telephones and faxes to coordinate some of its more remote service providers who do not even have access to computers. Managers who use the lack of technology as an excuse for not pursuing these strategies today may find themselves vulnerable to more aggressive competitors who figure out how to work around the constraints imposed by existing technologies.

Nevertheless, although new technology is not necessary, new generations of information technology can be extraordinarily helpful in accelerating the movement toward leveraged growth and in capturing even more value from these initiatives. Li & Fung employees today spend a significant amount of their time manually collecting performance data from their service providers and disseminating information back to service providers regarding specific process assignments. Imagine the effort that could be saved if automated information connections could be quickly established and maintained at a low cost across process networks. The tasks performed by Li & Fung employees could be substantially upgraded, the employees would move from routine information management to much more high value consultative work, and the company would help service providers use performance information to more rapidly upgrade their capabilities.

Web services technology can play a key role in supporting integrated growth strategies in general. Organic growth is often held back by a lack of flexibility in IT systems. Introducing new product lines, adding specialized services around existing product lines, or even expanding through the addition of new sales channels can often take much longer because of the lead times to add new functionality to IT systems. Web services technology can help by providing a lower-cost and more flexible way to access new functionality and combine it with the functionality of existing systems. Chapter 2 already discussed the challenges of postmerger integration of IT systems. By helping to combine existing IT systems in a faster, more targeted way than would be possible with previous generations of technology, Web services technology can improve a company's ability to reap business value from postmerger operations. Finally, Web services technology can deepen the ability to execute leveraged growth strategies. At the outset, leveraged growth hinges on the ability to establish flexible and low-cost connections with a growing array of enterprises. In the longer term, amplifying the economic value generated by leveraged growth requires a systematic capturing of performance information and the dissemination of that information in ways that help participants accelerate their performance improvement initiatives. In both the early stages and later stages of leveraged growth strategies, Web services technology can significantly reduce the cost and increase the effectiveness of the information flows required to drive economic value creation.

At the other extreme, one would be equally mistaken to view information technology as sufficient to execute successful leveraged growth strategies. Leveraged growth strategies ultimately depend on a sophisticated understanding of the economic incentives required to mobilize assets owned by others. To be successful, these strategies must include an understanding of what customers value, since this ultimately generates any economic incentives that can be offered to third parties. Finally, companies pursuing these leveraged growth strategies must have a clear view of how they can capture for themselves a significant portion of the value generated. Information technology can be a significant enabler of leveraged growth strategies, but the strategies themselves must be sound in order to create and capture economic value.

Leveraged growth strategies also require a very different kind of organization. Organizational capabilities like performance measurement and rewards systems often prove to be the key obstacle in moving to more aggressive leveraged growth strategies. Chapter 9 focuses on some of the organizational changes required to exploit the growth potential created by Web services technology.

9

Reconfiguring
the Organization

THERE IS NO DOUBT that businesses must respond to intensifying competition and deliver higher levels of profitability and growth. These needs in turn require a much higher degree of flexibility and collaboration. The good news is that emerging information technology provides a necessary platform—previous generations of technology simply were not up to the task. Management needs to implement new business approaches—process networks, unbundling, and leveraged growth—to exploit the economic opportunities created by this new information technology. The vision is attractive, but can it be executed?

Economic success will only be possible if management reconfigures the organization to address these opportunities. Very different ways of organizing will be required. Understanding the new ways of organizing is only part of the challenge. The dead ends and land mines along the path from here to there will undermine the efforts of the most visionary management. The challenges along the way will ultimately lead most companies down the path to value destruction rather than value creation.

Unless they confront and deal with these challenges, companies will experience only marginal near-term performance improvement from this new generation of technology. Organization becomes an increasingly significant roadblock to further performance improvement—in terms of either profitability or growth. In particular, any effort to implement more aggressive growth strategies will require focused attention to profound organizational change. If management cannot overcome this roadblock, the company will become increasingly vulnerable to more aggressive competitors. Near-term performance improvement will eventually give way to performance erosion.

A very different approach to business strategy development will be required to navigate successfully down the right path. Layered approaches to strategy will provide the necessary compass to help management deal with the enormous complexity and uncertainty involved in reconfiguring the organization. Layered strategies will in turn lead to layered organizational change, helping to tighten the link between organizational change and business impact. Rather than trying to reconfigure the organization all at once, this approach seeks to implement organizational change in rapid increments explicitly tied to aggressive performance objectives.

Layered Strategies

Layered strategies challenge conventional wisdom about business strategy on two dimensions. Read most standard strategy texts, and two basic principles come through loud and clear. First, management must invest significant time and effort to define a detailed business strategy based on rigorous, fact-based analysis before moving into the implementation phase. Second, the relevant time frame for strategy development is a five-year horizon, leading to the well-known five-year plan with detailed initiatives laid out for each year and equally detailed financial projections quantifying the financial impact of these initiatives.

Layered strategies take a different approach. They begin with the assumption that strategy development and implementation cannot be done sequentially but instead must proceed roughly in parallel, with each layer of initiative shaping the other as the process unfolds. Sequential approaches work well in relatively stable environments. As change accelerates and uncertainty about outcomes increases, sequential approaches become less helpful. Emphasis on detailed and rigorous, fact-based analysis quickly leads to analysis paralysis as management decides to wait until the

FIGURE 9 - 1

Layered Strategies for Reconfiguring a Business

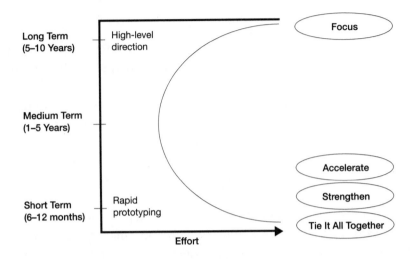

changes unfold and the "facts" become clearer. Or, if a company is under pressure for action, the sequential approach can lead to misguided strategies based upon "facts" that soon become obsolete.

Layered strategies also operate on different time horizons. Rather than focusing on a one- to five-year time horizon, layered strategies concentrate on both a longer and shorter time horizon. One layer of initiative concentrates on framing a view of the future that typically looks beyond five years and may sometimes extend over several decades. A second and third layer of initiative concentrates on a much shorter time horizon, typically six to twelve months. With this approach, management spends very little time on the one- to five-year time horizon, which becomes largely irrelevant. All of management attention tends to switch back and forth between a much longer and a much shorter time horizon.

What are the various layers of strategy development, and how do they relate to each other? The layers can be summarized by a FAST acronym: focus, accelerate, strengthen, and tie it all together. Figure 9-1 shows these layers arrayed against two key time horizons: long term (five to ten years) and short term (six to twelve months). The figure suggests that management must concentrate its attention and effort against these two time horizons and invest much less effort on issues in the one- to five-year time horizon.

Focus: Defining the Direction

The first layer of strategy development is in some respects the most challenging. In the face of enormous uncertainty, it requires senior management and ultimately the entire organization to align around a common view of the long-term future and its implications for economic value creation. The natural temptation of senior management is to avoid this requirement. "The future is too uncertain. We have enough difficulty anticipating what the market will look like one year from now—how can we possibly anticipate what it will look like five to ten years from now?"

This reaction is completely understandable. There are two responses. First, the consequences of avoiding this requirement can be devastating. Second, the requirement may not be as daunting as it first seems.

If senior management does not align around a common view of the long-term future, then corporations can quickly fall into a reactive posture. Since accelerating change creates a broad range of challenges and opportunities, companies without a clear sense of long-term direction tend to quickly lose focus, spreading their resources too thinly across too many initiatives.

This absence of long-term focus has two consequences. Without any ability to prioritize initiatives, it becomes very difficult to mobilize a critical mass of resources behind any of the initiatives, leading to suboptimal performance across all the initiatives. Second, because there are so many initiatives under way, it is difficult to create any sense of urgency if some initiatives begin to fail. Senior management tends to become complacent—if some initiatives are failing, not to worry, because there are many others that may yet succeed.

The bottom line is this: A vicious cycle emerges as performance begins to deteriorate and more initiatives are launched to expand options, leading to further deterioration in performance. In many respects, this was the fate experienced by many dot-coms that went to market with no clear idea of their destination. The mantra was,

Get into the market quickly, and figure it out along the way. The result? Efforts were fragmented, resource requirements mounted, and performance deteriorated until investors lost patience and the funds ran out.

Large companies are only somewhat less vulnerable. They usually have more resources and a core business that continues to move forward, at least in the short term. Take any major business imperative—cost reduction, new product introduction, international expansion, or others. Then do an audit of the initiatives within the company that are focused on one of these imperatives. Chances are, you will find that the senior management has no idea of the full range of initiatives under way across the company. You will probably also find that management is surprised at the magnitude of the resources being deployed in aggregate across all these initiatives and is sorely disappointed at the limited impact being generated.

Significant penalties thus accrue with the lack of long-term direction. On the other hand, the task of defining a long-term direction may not be as difficult as initially thought. In contrast to traditional approaches to strategic planning, the layered approach does not require a detailed view of the future. Instead, it requires a relatively high-level view that is broad enough to accommodate many variations in outcome, but specific enough to help make choices and prioritize business initiatives in the near term. Defining the strategic direction in too much detail tends to reduce flexibility and lock the business in too tightly to one narrow outcome. On the other hand, if the direction is framed too broadly, it does not help management make difficult, near-term choices.

Let's look at a specific example. Despite significant controversy, Microsoft remains a leading example of a company that has created substantial economic value in a rapidly changing and highly uncertain market. Early on, Bill Gates defined a compelling long-term direction for Microsoft. The direction could be summarized in two succinct sentences: "Computing power is inexorably moving from large, centralized mainframes to distributed desktops. To create significant economic value in this market, companies must establish leadership positions in desktop technology." The first sentence summarized a view of the future of the computer industry. The second sentence made explicit the implications for what kind of business Microsoft would need to build to be successful in this market. Developed in the late 1970s, Gates's definition of a strategic direction was not a five-year direction, but a direction that served the company well for two decades.

The direction did not offer great detail, but it was sufficient to help Microsoft prioritize its response to market opportunities. Microsoft began by marketing a version of the BASIC programming language. This product had become very popular among early adopters of the microprocessor-based computers that were beginning to populate the desktop. When IBM called Microsoft one day to inquire if it would be interested in developing an operating system for a new desktop computer that IBM was planning to market, senior management knew that this was a significant opportunity to accelerate its movement toward a leadership position on the desktop. Luck certainly played a role. IBM had initially approached another company with this opportunity, but that company (Digital Research) delayed in responding. Microsoft responded quickly and mobilized a concerted effort precisely because it knew that this opportunity was very consistent with its long-term direction.

Defining such a long-term direction can be challenging, even if the details don't have to be filled in. Many companies like Wal-Mart, TCI, and Microsoft met the challenge by rallying around the vision of the founder who played a strong leadership role in the company. Other companies have tended to fall in line behind an industry shaper and appropriated the long-term direction of the shaper as their own. These adapters then identify complementary capabilities that they must develop in order to create value around the industry shaper. Companies like Dell, Solectron, and Intuit have created large and profitable businesses by understanding unmet market needs created by the initiatives of shapers.

In the absence of a strong founder/leader or other corporate shaper, senior management will need to devote significant time as a leadership team to define and agree upon a long-term direction. Scenario development tools can be very helpful in supporting this process. Management can use these tools to more systematically understand the full spectrum of uncertainty regarding potential outcomes. It then has a structured process to converge on the most likely outcome and its implications for the company.

These tools are particularly helpful in making explicit key assumptions behind alternative views of the future. As it becomes clear which assumptions are most critical to specific outcomes, management can begin to identify events or data that might serve as leading indicators to test the validity of these assumptions. For example, one company discovered that early customer behavior on the Internet could provide significant insight into the long-term attractiveness of certain business models. Early tendencies to return repeatedly to a limited number of Web sites for purchases might diminish the long-term attractiveness of portals and increase the value of broad-based retail sites. In some cases, management may also discover initiatives their company can take to increase the likelihood of one preferred outcome. If the company wished to shift this early behavior to favor more active surfing across a broader range of sites, it might develop better navigation tools to make the search for specific products more convenient.

The point is that companies need a clear and compelling, but not too detailed, view of their long-term direction. This direction is critical to making difficult choices regarding the deployment of resources in the near term. Precisely because these choices are so difficult, the long-term direction must be deeply shared by the entire senior management team. Building this deeply shared view is difficult and time-consuming. For this reason, scenario development tools and other approaches to building shared understanding among senior management can be helpful to ensure that the entire senior management team is on board.

If the perspective in this book is correct, senior management will need to reassess the long-term direction of the company at a fundamental level. Many questions need to be asked. Has senior management undertaken this reassessment? What role did technologists who deeply understand these new technologies play in pushing management to question key assumptions about its business? In assessing implications, did management question whether the boundaries of existing markets or industries would be reshaped by these new technologies? What process networks or economic webs will likely be important to the company in the decades ahead? What role will the company play in these process networks or economic webs? Where will profits migrate as Web services architectures evolve? What early milestones in the development of these technologies and architectures can provide management with better insight regarding the direction and pace of technology-enabled business change?

Accelerate: Moving the Business

As senior management defines a long-term direction, it can begin to reassess key operating initiatives in the business. In this layer of strategy development, the time horizon compresses dramatically to six to twelve months. The challenge here is to determine what can be done to move even faster over the next six to twelve months toward the long-term direction. Rapid prototyping describes the management mind-set in this time horizon—what can be done quickly to test and refine approaches to near-term business opportunities?

Questions to be asked in this layer of strategy development include the following: Which operational initiatives have the greatest potential to advance the business toward the long-term direction? Do these initiatives have enough critical mass to ensure high impact? Are there other operational initiatives that the company could be launching in the near term to accelerate impact? What can be done to make the high-priority operational initiatives even more effective? Are other less important operational initiatives diverting resources?

In one dimension, this layer involves restructuring the portfolio of near-term operational initiatives to ensure that the appropriate initiatives are receiving the necessary support and that the company is not spreading its resources too broadly. In another dimension, this layer involves continually reexamining high-priority initiatives to determine if they can be reconfigured so that they deliver even more impact, more quickly. Strategic direction-setting heavily shapes this layer, although it requires much more tactical, operational expertise.

Specifically in the context of our technology discussion, managers need to look at how to address near-term initiatives to implement Web services technology and how to capture the operating savings. Chances are that most large companies today have some initiatives already under way in this area. Does senior management know the range of initiatives? Which initiatives have the greatest potential to deliver tangible near-term operating savings? Are there other initiatives that might be easier to implement while delivering even larger savings? Could the size, timing, or probability of the savings be enhanced by more focused resource deployments? Are these initiatives structured so that clear, near-term operational milestones can provide evidence of progress and impact? Are business line managers appropriately involved in shaping these initiatives and evaluating key milestones? Is the company making the necessary changes in business operations to maximize the potential impact of this technology?

Look again at Microsoft. The company has long had a bias for action. The priority for management is to get into the market quickly and then, in light of market feedback, refine along the way. Early-stage product initiatives often perform very poorly in the market, but management rapidly refines products according to performance feedback until the products achieve leadership positions. Management continually reassesses key operating initiatives both in terms of near-term performance and ability to contribute to the long-term direction. If poorly performing initiatives are central to the long-term direction of the company, they are aggressively reworked until they perform well. If they are less central, they are shut down and the resources reallocated to higher-potential operating initiatives.

Strengthen: Enhancing Organizational Capabilities

A third layer of strategy operates on the same time horizon as the "accelerate" layer—six to twelve months. In this layer, management seeks to identify major organizational roadblocks that are hampering even more rapid execution of high-priority operational initiatives. It then launches a series of near-term initiatives to remove or reduce the impact of these roadblocks. Again, the focus is on very tactical performance—what impact can be achieved in the next six to twelve months? The organizational initiatives are explicitly linked to near-term operational initiatives that in turn have been prioritized based on long-term strategic direction. As a result, these are tightly focused organizational initiatives designed to help accelerate near-term movement toward a long-term strategic direction.

The organizational obstacles can take many forms. The company may not have enough people with the right kinds of skills. Information systems may not be producing appropriate or reliable information. Performance measurement and incentive systems may be misaligned with key operating objectives. Reporting relationships may not be appropriately structured. Information technology platforms may be too rigid to permit rapid response to changing market conditions. The obstacles may be enormous and ultimately require massive organizational change. Nevertheless, the initiatives to address these obstacles are always focused on near-term impact and tightly linked to key operational initiatives.

Microsoft again illustrates this approach. Senior management puts enormous priority on recruiting programs to strengthen organizational capabilities, but recruiting efforts are tightly linked to specific operating initiatives. Management frequently reorganizes the company to respond to near-term needs and then reorganizes again when these near-term needs change.

In seeking to enhance organizational capabilities, especially in the short term, it becomes important not to focus exclusively on internal capabilities. Often, building these capabilities internally can require significant lead times and resource commitments. Management must continuously wrestle with make-versus-buy choices in strengthening organizational capability—should the capability be built internally or sourced externally?

These choices are particularly difficult if there is insufficient alignment around long-term strategic direction. To use the terms popularized by Geoffrey Moore, we must ask, Which capabilities are truly *core* in the sense that they are critical to the long-term sustainability of the business? Which capabilities are *context* and should be sourced externally if reasonable options can be found?

Again, Microsoft has proven to be adept at augmenting its own organizational capabilities with complementary resources provided by others. Over time, it has shaped a broad web of businesses that support and add value to its technology architecture. Specialized application software providers, peripherals vendors, resellers, consultants, and systems-integration firms all complement the capabilities of Microsoft itself. Microsoft can move more quickly because it can rely on these other companies for specialized capabilities. It can also focus its own organizational capabilities even more tightly on areas that are truly central to its long-term strategic direction.

A later section, Layered Organizational Change, lays out a broad migration path for organizational change shaped by the adoption of Web services technology. At a more tactical level, senior managers should be challenging the organization to ensure that it has deep enough skills in Web services technology to maximize the impact of near-term operational initiatives deploying this technology. Managers need to consider several questions: If the skills are not sufficient in the organization, are there third parties that can provide transitional access to the necessary skills as the organization fills in with targeted hiring and development plans? Do business line managers have a deep enough understanding of the changes required in the business to exploit the technology? If not, what can be done in terms of targeted learning to build this understanding in the next six months? To the extent that these near-term operational initiatives extend to include other companies, do other companies have compelling incentives to move as quickly as possible to support these initiatives? What additional incentives can management implement to accelerate the initiatives by these other companies? Who is accountable for the performance of these interenterprise initiatives, and do they have the necessary skills to deliver results in a timely manner? Are the mechanisms in place to capture and disseminate the learning generated by the current wave of operational initiatives?

Tie It All Together: Integrating Waves of Initiatives

The fourth layer is perhaps most important of all. It requires management to rapidly iterate across all layers and to continuously refine the initiatives in each layer through the insights gained in all layers. Doing this requires management to zoom in and zoom out in rapid succession, often in the course of a single meeting. Zooming in involves getting deeply involved in detailed discussions of near-term operating and organizational initiatives. Zooming out involves pulling back to explore the implications for long-term strategic direction. Through these approaches, management seeks to build robust feedback loops connecting each layer, so that the experience gained in one layer can help shape initiatives in every other layer.

Long-term strategic direction does not simply focus near-term initiatives. Management can gain significant insight into its long-term strategic direction from experiences gained in managing near-term operating and organizational initiatives. Moving into markets, building operating experience, and removing the bottlenecks for organizations—these steps provide constant learning that can help refine long-term strategic direction. Feedback loops are not just operating in one direction.

Management can foster this interaction across layers by fashioning waves of activity that move in parallel along layers simultaneously. These waves of activity are typically short-lived—six months, perhaps twelve months. They provide an opportunity to define specific performance milestones across the organization, helping senior management measure progress within each layer. These waves also encourage the organization to step back at regular intervals and synthesize new learning from the day-to-day experiences within each layer.

In the context of Web services, these waves of initiatives will usually vary in detail, but often fit into some broad patterns. Early waves are likely to be focused on the edge of the enterprise, helping deliver tangible, near-term operating savings by addressing inefficiencies in business processes that reach into business partners. Subsequent waves will begin to move in two directions—back into the enterprise and farther out along relevant process networks to embrace a broader range of business participants. Increasingly, the waves will expand their focus from targeted operational performance improvements to broader structural changes designed to position the enterprise to capture further operating savings as well as significant growth potential. Even later waves will focus on delivering accelerating growth.

Layered Organizational Change

Management faces an enormous challenge in reconfiguring organizations from hardwired models to much more loosely coupled, dynamically reconfigured models. All the dimensions of the organ-

FIGURE 9 - 2

Migration Path of Layered Organizational Change

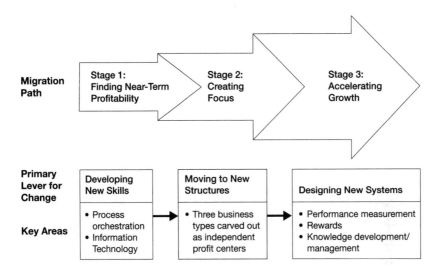

ization will need to undergo fundamental change. The full migration is likely to take decades, and the ultimate organizational forms are barely understood today. They are likely to vary significantly across the three types of businesses discussed earlier—customer relationship businesses, infrastructure management businesses, and product innovation and commercialization businesses.

Creating a detailed road map of organizational change would be an exercise in futility, much in the same way that detailed strategic plans are less and less helpful to management. Instead, management needs a broad outline of the changes ahead and some sense of the rough sequencing of organizational change initiatives. Not surprisingly, this broad outline can track closely to the three stages of migration discussed throughout the book (figure 9-2).

At each stage of migration, a different dimension, or layer, of the organization becomes the primary lever for change. In the first stage, skills become the primary lever for change. In the second stage, organizational structure replaces skills as the primary lever. In the third stage, systems emerge as the primary lever. Each of these primary levers of change will catalyze supporting changes in other layers of the organization.

Stage 1: Finding Near-Term Profitability—
Developing New Skills

In the first stage of migration, building skills becomes a primary focus of organizational change. Two types of skills are particularly important to complete this stage successfully—early process orchestration skills and distributed service architecture skills.

As discussed earlier, in this stage, much of the business focus is on improving operating performance at the edge of the enterprise by the use of new Web services technology to enhance coordination across enterprises. To do this effectively, companies must begin to designate process orchestrators. These are senior executives who will be held accountable for the performance of a business process that extends beyond the boundaries of the enterprise to encompass activities within other companies. The three core processes within a company—supply-chain management, customer relationship management, and product innovation and commercialization—typically extend outward to involve other enterprises. Process orchestrators can be designated for one or more of these core processes.

Many companies have already developed "process owner" roles, but these roles typically stop at the boundary of the enterprise. In most cases, these process owners will expand their roles to become process orchestrators. By moving beyond the boundary of the enterprise, though, process orchestrators will require a broader skill set.

For example, imagine a process orchestrator for supply-chain management. This person would be held accountable for reducing operating expense and inventory levels by enhancing coordination with suppliers and logistics providers along the entire value chain. The authority of the process orchestrator stops at the edge of the enterprise, but somehow the orchestrator must persuade numerous other companies to adopt a variety of policies, practices, and platforms to improve process efficiency.

To do this effectively, process orchestrators need to have a reasonably deep understanding of the different kinds of businesses involved, both in terms of the economics that drive those businesses and in terms of the capabilities required for success. The process orchestrator needs to understand what will motivate other companies to adopt something new. In many respects, process orchestrators must act as managers of organizational change, with the key new wrinkle that the change must be coordinated across multiple organizations. The process orchestrator cannot dictate action. Instead, this person must build trust and put into place appropriate incentives for action. These initiatives will have to be staged. Relatively modest commitments at the outset can generate tangible value and motivate the participants to undertake more significant changes.

In this respect, one of the first steps that Li & Fung, the company introduced in chapter 8, took to shift from a traditional Chinese trading company to a focused orchestrator involved hiring a new cadre of managers. These managers had previous work experience in apparel operations like the ones in the companies Li & Fung sought to recruit into its process network. These individuals had a deep understanding of the work processes required to produce a garment, could quickly evaluate the capabilities of an apparel operation, and understood what it would take to motivate these operations to perform to increasingly demanding specifications.

Process orchestrators also need to be information architects. To coordinate activity across enterprises, they must understand what information is essential and structure these information flows to ensure efficient and reliable activity.

This leads to the second set of key skills required in this migration stage: distributed service architecture skills. Typically, process orchestrators will not possess these skills themselves. They will need to be teamed up with a senior IT executive—a distributed services architect—who can help design and implement the appropriate IT platforms to support process orchestration across enterprises. As discussed, Web services technology is a fundamentally new generation of technology. Very few organizations yet possess the skills required to implement this technology, much less the sophisticated new architectures required to harness the capability of the technology.

Distributed service architects are critical if a company wishes to understand the current capabilities of Web services technology. What is perhaps even more important, these architects must also have a clear sense of the current limitations of the technology. Web services technology is rapidly evolving. To ensure that the capabilities of the technology are being fully utilized and do not exceed the limits of current functionality, the architects must carefully stage these technology implementations (and related business initiatives).

Distributed service architects will also need to work with IT departments to ensure that a broader set of Web services technology skills are available to support the implementation and operation of Web services platforms. The skills can be sourced externally at least initially, but most large companies will need to build appropriate internal capabilities in this critical technology as well.

Perhaps one of the biggest challenges of distributed service architects will be to act as knowledge brokers. They must first of all bridge the gap between business managers and IT managers, working closely with process orchestrators to shape the business initiatives, given the capabilities and limitations of the technology. At the same time, they will confront an equally challenging gap within the IT organization. To work effectively, Web services technology must be grafted onto existing legacy applications. Few people will possess the appropriate technological skill in both legacy technologies and Web services technology. Teams of people possessing the necessary range of IT skills will need to come together and work effectively to begin the migration toward a Web services architecture.

Building these broad new skill sets within the organization will in turn require other supporting organizational changes. For example, the development of process orchestration skills will typically require a company to define new roles, craft new reporting relationships, modify performance measurement and reward systems, and design new information systems. Senior managers can focus all these organizational changes using the FAST framework outlined earlier. They will need to answer questions like these: What are the necessary skills in performance orchestration and Web services technology to support very specific near-term operating initiatives designed to yield tangible, near-term economic results? What supporting organizational changes are required to accelerate the building of these new skills and the generation of tangible business impact?

Stage 2: Creating Focus—Moving to New Structures

In the second stage of the migration path, the focus of the organizational change shifts to a significant restructuring of the enterprise. This is the stage of aggressive unbundling of business activity to create more focused growth platforms. New organizational structures will be required to support this process.

To begin with, most enterprises will need to structurally segment the three business types—customer relationship businesses, infrastructure management businesses, and product innovation and commercialization businesses—operating within their company. Today, because the structures of most enterprises do not map easily to these three business types, the performance of these types tends to be suboptimized. Whether or not senior management decides to focus exclusively on one business type, it should at least try to create more focused organizational homes for each type.

While easy to specify in theory, in practice this is perhaps the most challenging—and risky—phase in the organizational migration. We are now dealing with the core economics of the enterprise and parceling out these economics in a fundamentally new way. The potential for the disruption of operations is large. It is also easy to miss or underestimate the importance of economic interdependencies across these three business types. Unless this interdependence is made explicit and organizational mechanisms established to deal with them, the long-term economic performance of the business may suffer. The economics are challenging enough. Add complex personal and organizational dynamics as major parts of the business are torn apart and recombined, and you have a minefield where each step can lead to a major explosion.

To manage this risk, a company must start with a pivotal role—the creation of business-type managers. These business-type managers would provide the focal point for restructuring to bring together in one place all the business activities for each of the business types.

Imagine how this might play out in a retail bank, for example. Most retail banks today have managers responsible for addressing particular customer segments, such as wealthy individuals or small

businesses. These managers would gain considerably more authority in their new role as business-type managers. They could determine what channels they wanted to use to reach their customer
segment, whether or not the channels were provided by the bank.
They could source financial service products from a variety of
sources and would have broader ability to shape the marketing and
sales programs required to reach their customer segment.

On the other hand, these customer relationship business managers would not have direct management responsibility for the
operations of call centers or branch bank facilities, even though
these operations are essential to customer relations. These facilities,
along with a variety of back-office processing operations like check
processing or mortgage loan processing, would be operated by
infrastructure business managers. These managers could also execute make-versus-buy decisions, deciding in some cases to outsource their operations to more specialized providers. They would
also have the ability to offer their operations to other banks on an
outsourced basis.

Product innovation and commercialization business managers
would be responsible for creating new financial service products.
They would have the growing freedom to market their products
through other customer relationship businesses. They would have
to negotiate to gain access to necessary infrastructure management
services from the infrastructure business managers within the bank
or from more specialized providers outside the bank.

As might be imagined, many existing operations that are run as
cost centers would now be positioned as profit centers. Certainly
each of the business type managers would be expected to operate
his or her operations as profit centers. To carry out this performance objective, the business-type managers would have greater
freedom to offer their services to other companies or to source services from other companies. The process orchestrators described in
the previous section would help mobilize third-party resources to
support business types.

The IT organization would itself fragment more explicitly into
the three business types. One group within the IT organization—
the customer relationship component—would have responsibility

for working with other parts of the business to define IT needs and to source those needs from the most qualified providers, whether or not they were part of the bank's IT department. Another group—the product innovation and commercialization component—would specialize in rapid and efficient development of IT applications and platforms, potentially for other customers outside the bank. A third group—the infrastructure management component—would operate IT platforms on behalf of users, whether or not they are part of the bank.

These focused business entities might all continue to be owned by the enterprise that spawned them, although operated as independent business units. More likely, however, most of these entities would ultimately be spun off as independent companies, leaving the enterprise eventually focused on only one business type. This one business type would then become the platform for accelerated growth in the final stage of migration.

Li & Fung's decision to reorganize around customer units represented one of the key turning points in the evolution of the company. By firmly establishing the customer relationship managers as the key decision makers in the organization, Li & Fung declared its identity going forward. It would be a customer relationship business, rather than an infrastructure management business. It would rely on others to provide infrastructure management operations—its key value added would be in understanding customer needs and helping customers connect with the right bundle of resources to serve those needs.

As discussed, although structure would be the primary lever of organizational change in this second stage, changes in structure would have profound ripple effects, requiring many other changes throughout the organization. Business-type managers would require an increasingly focused set of skills to effectively run much more specialized, independent businesses. Performance measurement and reward systems would need to be tailored to support the unique needs of each type of business. Information systems would need to be modified to provide business-type managers with relevant information. As discussed in chapter 7, each of the business types would develop distinctive organizational cultures and styles.

Stage 3: Accelerating Growth—Designing New Systems

In the third stage of migration, the focus of organizational change shifts again, this time to the design of new systems—performance measurement, reward, knowledge development and management, and information systems. To successfully exploit the economic potential available at this stage, senior managers will need to evolve to organizational forms that effectively coordinate activity across a broad range of dynamically configured service providers. Coordination ability will be either enhanced or hampered by organizational systems. As indicated in chapter 8, Li & Fung is now focused on taking informal systems and implementing more systematic, automated platforms to capture performance information and to use this to enhance the performance of its process network.

Dynamic configuration of service providers within a process network requires finely tuned performance measurement systems that can reach out across multiple entities. If Li & Fung is in discussion with an apparel designer regarding men's gabardine slacks, the company needs to ask, Who are the best suppliers and the best cutters of this kind of fabric? Who will do best at sewing and assembling men's gabardine slacks? If lead times are even more important than usual and the customer is willing to accept higher costs, who can best meet these performance parameters? As discussed in chapters 6 and 8, the ability of the process network to deliver value to customers hinges on a detailed, real-time view of the performance of various participants. Li & Fung does this extremely well today because its staff has developed a deep understanding of the performance capabilities of its service providers. The company believes that it will do it even better with more automated systems.

The ability to mobilize appropriate service providers on a timely basis will depend on tailored reward systems based on a deep understanding of the different types of companies involved. Generating significant economic value in this stage will require the ability to deepen knowledge rapidly across multiple service providers. Only in this way will performance continue to improve so that there is a bigger economic pie to allocate among the business participants. This will require much more robust knowledge development systems as well as knowledge management systems.

In focusing on systems, a business must keep in mind that organizational systems can be enhanced by information technology, but not reduced to information technology. Organizational systems require policies, procedures, and people to operate effectively. Particularly in the case of knowledge development and knowledge management, deep understanding of how people interact with each other and with their work will be key to enhancing performance. In many respects, this understanding will ultimately be the key to unlocking the economic value potential of loosely coupled business operations. Without a rapid deepening of knowledge and more effective access to that knowledge, businesses will largely be restricted to capturing efficiency savings from a fixed pool of value. Li & Fung deeply understands this point. Despite more aggressive efforts to harness information technology to support its organizational performance, the senior management remains committed to the view that improved knowledge ultimately comes from people working together. Organizational initiatives in this area are focused on creating opportunities for the right people to come together at appropriate times to explore ways to enhance operating performance.

At this early stage, we can only start to speculate about the organizational forms that will evolve. These organizational forms will need to address the opportunities and cope with the challenges involved in mobilizing resources, regardless of where they reside.

The very definition of an organization as a distinct entity will be challenged. What used to be "inside" the organization will be broadly available to others. Similarly, what used to be "outside" the organization will be increasingly accessible to support key business objectives. At one level, these new forms of organization will be quite large and concentrated (as is likely to be the case in customer relationship businesses and infrastructure management businesses). Consequently, they will bear little resemblance to visions of virtual organizations, with no assets and few people. On the other hand, their reach will be even broader as they mobilize the resources of others. They will be a curious mix of very physical and virtual entities, rapidly evolving to exploit new economic opportunities.

Like everything else in business, we can only begin to imagine the broad outlines of what will evolve. Above all, we should not let that hold us back from beginning the migration to much more focused, high-growth businesses. Don't be distracted by visions that require large, up-front investments with economic payoffs far in the future. More often than not, these visions prove to be mirages, destroying enormous economic value.

The key will be to move incrementally and pragmatically, but rapidly. Each step along the migration path should yield tangible, near-term business value. In the process, each step will yield significant learning, and the destination will become progressively clearer.

Epilogue

Staying Connected

BOOKS ALLOW both the author and the reader to explore a broad terrain in some detail. They provide a roadmap that can help busy executives cope better with the daily pressures of running a business. Books help executives make connections among what at first seem to be isolated events. They also offer a deeper understanding of the actions that must be taken to continue to create economic value.

On the other hand, books do not cope well with rapidly changing business environments. The frustration of authors is that months, if not years, pass between the time they submit a manuscript and the time a reader actually picks up the book to read it. The frustration of readers is that they receive a snapshot of events that continue to evolve rapidly without a clear sense of what has changed and what has remained the same.

Fortunately, the advent of the Internet helps remedy this limitation. Readers interested in staying up-to-date on the trends discussed in this book are invited to visit my Web site at www.johnhagel.com. While visiting there, readers will also be able to subscribe to my forthcoming newsletter. Perhaps in this way, we will be able to continue together the journey that begins—but only begins—with this book.

Further Reading

Arthur, Brian. "Increasing Returns and the New World of Business." *Harvard Business Review*, July–August 1996, 100–109.

———. *Increasing Returns and Path Dependence in the Economy*. Ann Arbor: University of Michigan Press, 1994.

Auguste, Byron G., Yvonne Hao, Marc Singer, and Michael Wiegand. "The Other Side of Outsourcing." *McKinsey Quarterly*, no. 1 (2002): 52–63.

Axelrod, Robert. *The Complexity of Cooperation: Agent-Based Models of Competition and Collaboration*. Princeton: Princeton University Press, 1997.

Baldwin, Carliss Y., and Kim B. Clark. *Design Rules*. Vol. 1, *The Power of Modularity*. Cambridge, MA: MIT Press, 2000.

Barney, Jay B., and William G. Ouchi, eds. *Organizational Economics: Toward a New Paradigm for Understanding and Studying Organizations*. San Francisco: Jossey-Bass, 1988.

Beinhocker, Eric D. "Strategy at the Edge of Chaos." *McKinsey Quarterly*, no. 1 (1997): 24–39.

Birch, David J., and Eileen Burnett-Kant. "Unbundling the Unbundled." *McKinsey Quarterly*, no. 4 (2001): 102–111.

Blackwell, Roger D. *From Mind to Market: Reinventing the Retail Supply Chain*. New York: HarperBusiness, 1997.

Boisot, Max H. *Information Space: A Framework for Learning in Organizations, Institutions, and Culture*. London: Routledge, 1995.

Bradley, Stephen P., and Richard L. Nolan. *Sense & Respond: Capturing Value in the Network Era*. Boston: Harvard Business School Press, 1998.

Brandenburger, Adam M., and Barry J. Nalebuff. *Co-opetition: A Revolution Mind-Set That Combines Competition and Cooperation.* New York: Currency Doubleday, 1996.

Bresser, Rudi K. F., Michael A. Hitt, Robert D. Nixon, and Dieter Heuskel. *Winning Strategies in a Deconstructing World.* Chichester: John Wiley & Sons, 2000.

Britton, Chris. *IT Architectures and Middleware: Strategies for Building Large, Integrated Systems.* Boston: Addison-Wesley, 2001.

Brown, John Seely, ed. *Seeing Differently: Insights on Innovation.* Boston: Harvard Business School Press, 1997.

Brown, John Seely, and Paul Duguid. "Creativity versus Structure: A Useful Tension." *Sloan Management Review* 42, no. 4 (2001): 93–94.

———. "Knowledge and Organization: A Social-Practice Perspective." *Organization Science* 12, no. 2 (2001): 198–213.

———. "Organizational Learning and Communities of Practice: Towards a Unified View of Working, Learning and Innovation." *Organization Science* 2, no. 1 (1991): 40–58.

———. "Practice vs. Process: The Tension That Won't Go Away." *Knowledge Directions* (spring 2000): 86–96.

———. *The Social Life of Information.* Boston: Harvard Business School Press, 2000.

Brown, Shona, and Kathleen Eisenhardt. *Competing on the Edge: Strategy as Structured Chaos.* Boston: Harvard Business School Press, 1998.

Brynjolfsson, Erik, and Brian Kahin, eds. *Understanding the Digital Economy: Data, Tools, and Research.* Cambridge, MA: MIT Press, 2000.

Buchanan, James M., and Yong J. Yoon. *The Return to Increasing Returns.* Ann Arbor: University of Michigan Press, 1994.

Butler, Pat, Ted W. Hall, Alistair M. Hanna, Lenny Mendonca, Byron Auguste, James Manyika, and Anupam Sahay. "A Revolution in Interaction." *McKinsey Quarterly,* no. 1 (1997).

Cerami, Ethan. *Web Services Essentials.* Sebastopol, CA: O'Reilly & Associates, 2002.

Coase, R. H. *The Firm, the Market, and the Law.* Chicago: University of Chicago Press, 1988.

Copeland, Tom, and Vladimir Antikarov. *Real Options: A Practitioner's Guide.* New York: Texere, 2001.

Courtney, Hugh. *20/20 Foresight: Crafting Strategy in an Uncertain World.* Boston: Harvard Business School Press, 2001.

Coyne, Kevin P., and Somu Subramaniam. "Bringing Discipline to Strategy." *McKinsey Quarterly,* no. 4 (1996).

Davenport, Thomas H. *Mission Critical: Realizing the Promise of Enterprise Systems*. Boston: Harvard Business School Press, 2000.

Day, Jonathan D., and James C. Wendler. "The New Economics of Organization." *McKinsey Quarterly*, no. 1 (1998).

Dyer, Jeffrey H. *Collaborative Advantage: Winning through Extended Enterprise Supplier Networks*. Oxford: Oxford University Press, 2000.

Evans, Philip, and Thomas S. Wurster. *Blown to Bits: How the New Economics of Information Transforms Strategy*. Boston: Harvard Business School Press, 2000.

Fayad, Mohamed E., Douglas C. Schmidt, and Ralph E. Johnson. *Building Application Frameworks: Object-Oriented Foundations of Framework Design*. New York: John Wiley & Sons, 1999.

Fingar, Peter, and Ronald Aronica. *The Death of E and the Birth of the Real New Economy*. Tampa, FL: Meghan-Kiffer Press, 2001.

Foster, Richard, and Sarah Kaplan. *Creative Destruction: Why Companies That Are Built to Last Underperform the Market—and How to Successfully Transform Them*. New York: Currency, 2001.

Fukuyama, Francis. *Trust: The Social Virtues and the Creation of Prosperity*. New York: Free Press, 1995.

Gell-Man, Murray. *The Quark and the Jaguar: Adventures in the Simple and the Complex*. New York: W. H. Freeman, 1994.

Glass, Graham. *Web Services: Building Blocks for Distributed Systems*. Upper Saddle River, NJ: Prentice-Hall, 2000.

Hagel, John, III. "Spider vs. Spider." *McKinsey Quarterly*, no. 1 (1996) 4–18.

Hagel, John, III, and Arthur G. Armstrong. *Net Gain: Expanding Markets through Virtual Communities*. Boston: Harvard Business School Press, 1997.

Hagel, John, III, and John Seely Brown. "Cut Loose from Old Business Processes." *Optimize*, December 2001.

———. "Your Next IT Strategy." *Harvard Business Review*, October 2001, 105–113.

———. "Go Slowly with Web Services." *CIO*, 15 February 2002, 36–40.

Hagel, John, III, Todd Hewlin, and Todd Hutchings. "Retail Banking: Caught in a Web?" *McKinsey Quarterly*, no. 2 (1997): 42–54.

Hagel, John, III, and Jeffrey Rayport. "The Coming Battle for Customer Information." *Harvard Business Review*, January–February 1997, 53–65.

———. "The New Infomediaries." *McKinsey Quarterly*, no. 4 (1997): 54–70.

Hagel, John, III, and Toni Sacconaghi. "Who Will Benefit from Virtual Information?" *McKinsey Quarterly*, no. 3 (1996): 23–37.

Hagel, John, III, and Marc Singer. *Net Worth: Shaping Markets When Customers Make the Rules*. Boston: Harvard Business School Press, 1999.

———. "Unbundling the Corporation." *Harvard Business Review,* March–April 1999, 133–141.

Hixson, Richard F. *Privacy in a Public Society: Human Rights in Conflict.* New York: Oxford University Press, 1987.

Holland, John H. *Adaptation in Natural and Artificial Systems*. Ann Arbor: University of Michigan Press, 1975.

———. *Emergence: From Chaos to Order.* Reading, MA: Addison-Wesley, 1998.

———. *Hidden Order: How Adaptation Builds Complexity.* Reading, MA: Addison-Wesley, 1995.

Jasnowski, Mike. *Java, XML, and Web Services.* New York: Hungry Minds, 2002.

Jensen, Michael C. *A Theory of the Firm: Governance, Residual Claims, and Organizational Forms.* Cambridge, MA: Harvard University Press, 2000.

Johnson, George. *Fire in the Mind.* New York: Vintage, 1995.

Johnson, Steven. *Emergence: The Connected Lives of Ants, Brains, Cities, and Software.* New York: Scribner, 2001.

Kaplan, Steven N., ed. *Mergers and Productivity.* Chicago: University of Chicago Press, 2000.

Katz, Donald. *Just Do It: The Nike Spirit in the Corporate World.* Holbrook, MA: Adams Media Corporation, 1994.

Kauffman, Stuart. *At Home in the Universe: The Search for Laws of Self-Organization and Complexity.* New York: Oxford University Press, 1995.

———. "The Evolution of Economic Webs," in *The Economy as an Evolving Complex System,* edited by P. W. Anderson, K. J. Arrow, and D. Pines. Reading, MA: Addison-Wesley, 1988.

Kelly, Kevin. *Out of Control: The Rise of Neo-Biological Civilization.* Reading, MA: Addison-Wesley, 1994.

Klein, Daniel B. *Reputation: Studies in the Voluntary Elicitation of Good Conduct.* Ann Arbor: University of Michigan Press, 1997.

Lewis, William W., Vincent Palmade, Baudouin Regout, and Allen P. Webb. "What's Right with the U.S. Economy." *McKinsey Quarterly,* no. 1 (2002): 31–51.

Linthicum, David S. *B2B Application Integration: e-Business-Enable Your Enterprise.* Boston: Addison-Wesley, 2001.

Magretta, Joan. "Fast, Global, and Entrepreneurial: Supply Chain Management, Hong Kong Style—An Interview with Victor Fung." *Harvard Business Review,* September–October 1998, 103–114.

Malone, Thomas W., J. Yates, and R. I. Benjamin. "Electronic Markets and Electronic Hierarchies." *Communications of the ACM* 30, no. 6 (1987).

Manes, Stephen, and Paul Andrews. *Gates: How Microsoft's Mogul Reinvented an Industry—and Made Himself the Richest Man in America.* New York: Doubleday, 1993.

McGrath, James, Fritz Kroeger, Michael Traem, and Joerg Rockenhaeuser. *The Value Growers: Achieving Competitive Advantage through Long-term Growth and Profits.* New York: McGraw-Hill, 2001.

Moore, Geoffrey A. *Living on the Fault Line: Managing for Shareholder Value in the Age of the Internet.* New York: HarperBusiness, 2000.

Moore, James F. *The Death of Competition: Leadership and Strategy in the Age of Business Ecosystems.* New York: HarperBusiness, 1996.

Normann, Richard, and Rafael Ramirez. *Designing Interactive Strategy: From Value Chain to Value Constellation.* Chichester, England: John Wiley & Sons, 1994.

Oellermann, William L. *Architecting Web Services.* Berkeley: Apress, 2001.

Philips, Louis. *The Economics of Imperfect Information.* Cambridge: Cambridge University Press, 1988.

Pine, B. Joseph. *Mass Customization: The New Frontier in Business Competition.* Boston: Harvard Business School Press, 1993.

Poirier, Charles C., and Michael J. Bauer. *E-Supply Chain: Using the Internet to Revolutionize Your Business.* San Francisco: Berret-Koehler Publishers, 2000.

Quinn, James Bryan, Jordan J. Baruch, and Karen Anne Zien. *Innovation Explosion: Using Intellect and Software to Revolutionize Growth Strategies.* New York: The Free Press, 1997.

Quinn, James Bryan. *Intelligent Enterprise.* New York: The Free Press, 1992.

Randive, Vivek. *The Power of Now: How Winning Companies Sense and Respond to Change Using Real-Time Technology.* New York: McGraw-Hill, 1999.

Rauch, James E., and Alessandra Casella, eds. *Networks and Markets.* New York: Russell Sage Foundation, 2001.

Ruh, William A., Francis X. Maginnis, and William J. Brown. *Enterprise Application Integration.* New York: John Wiley & Sons, 2001.

Segel, Lee A., and Irun R. Cohen, eds. *Design Principles for the Immune System and Other Distributed Autonomous Systems.* Oxford: Oxford University Press, 2001.

Senge, Peter M. *The Fifth Discipline: The Art and Practice of the Learning Organization.* New York: Doubleday, 1990.

Shapiro, Carl, and Hal Varian. *Information Rules: A Strategic Guide to the Network Economy.* Boston: Harvard Business School Press, 1998.

Sirower, Mark L. *The Synergy Trap: Why Companies Lose the Acquisition Game.* New York: The Free Press, 1997.

Slywotzky, Adrian J., and David J. Morrison. *How Digital Is Your Business?* New York: Crown Business, 2000.

Stelter, Daniel, Mark Joiner, Eric Olsen, Neil Monnery, Xavier Mosquet, and Ahmed Fahour. *The Value Creators: A Study of the World's Top Performers.* Boston: Boston Consulting Group, 1999.

Strasser, J. B., and Laurie Becklund. *Swoosh: The Unauthorized Story of Nike and the Men Who Played There.* New York: HarperBusiness, 1991.

Treacy, Michael, and Fred Wiersema. *The Discipline of Market Leaders: Choose Your Customers, Narrow Your Focus, Dominate Your Market.* New York: Addison-Wesley Publishing, 1995.

Veryard, Richard. *The Component-Based Business: Plug and Play.* London: Springer, 2001.

Waldrop, W. Mitchell. *Complexity: The Emerging Science at the Edge of Order and Chaos.* New York: Touchstone, 1992.

Wallace, James, and Jim Erickson. *Hard Drive: Bill Gates and the Making of the Microsoft Empire.* New York: John Wiley & Sons, 1992.

Werbach, Kevin. "Web Services, Part I: Back to the Future of Software." *Release* 1.0, 20 September 2001, 1–21.

———. "Web Services, Part II: Back to the Future of Software." *Release* 1.0, 17 October 2001, 1–21.

Westin, Alan F. *Privacy and Freedom.* New York: Atheneum, 1967.

Westin, Alan F., and Michael A. Baker. *Databanks in a Free Society: Computers, Record-Keeping, and Privacy.* New York: Quadrangle Books, 1972.

Williamson, Oliver E. *The Economic Institutions of Capitalism.* New York: The Free Press, 1985.

———. *Markets and Hierarchies: Analysis and Antitrust Implications.* New York: Free Press, 1975.

———. *The Mechanisms of Governance.* Oxford: Oxford University Press, 1996.

Young, Fred. "Li & Fung." Case 9-301-009. Boston: Harvard Business School Publishing, 2000.

Zook, Chris, with James Allen. *Profit from the Core: Growth Strategy in an Era of Turbulence.* Boston: Harvard Business School Press, 2001.

Index

About the Author

John Hagel III is an independent business consultant who works with senior management to shape business strategies and improve business performance. He has spent the past two years helping to build entrepreneurial companies focused on commercializing Web services technology. Previously, he spent sixteen years with McKinsey & Company where he served as a leader of its Strategy Practice and founder and leader of its Electronic Commerce Practice. Prior to that, he served as Senior Vice President for strategic planning at Atari; as President of Sequoia Group, a systems house selling turn-key computer systems to physicians; and as a consultant with the Boston Consulting Group.

Hagel is an accomplished author. His two most recent books, *Net Gain: Expanding Markets through Virtual Communities* (coauthored with Arthur Armstrong) and *Net Worth: Shaping Markets When Customers Make the Rules* (coauthored with Marc Singer), were business book bestsellers and were translated into ten languages. He has written widely in the business press, including five articles for the *Harvard Business Review,* of which two won McKinsey Awards for best articles of the year.

Hagel lives in Silicon Valley in California with his wife and two daughters.

For more information about the author and his most recent perspectives, visit his Web site at www.johnhagel.com. His e-mail address is john@johnhagel.com.